wool pets

Making 20 Figures with Wool Roving and a Barbed Needle

Laurie Sharp

Photography by Kevin Sharp

Creative Publishing
international

This book is dedicated to "The Fab Four"—Hazel, Merna, Coco, and Carmella—my sheep.
They are a big part of my inspiration.

Creative Publishing
international

Copyright © 2008, Text, Laurie Sharp
Photographs, Kevin Sharp

ISBN-13: 978-1-58923-525-0
ISBN-10: 1-58923-525-8

10 9 8 7 6 5 4 3 2 1

Library of Congress Cataloging-in-Publication Data
Sharp, Laurie.
  Wool pets : making 20 figures with wool roving and a
barbed needle / by Laurie Sharp ; photography by Kevin
Sharp.
    p. cm.
  ISBN-13: 978-1-58923-385-0
  ISBN-10: 1-58923-385-9
  1. Felt work. 2. Felting. 3. Animals in art. I. Title.
  TT849.5.S53 2008
  746'.0463--dc22   2008000495
                                                CIP

Copy Editor: Sarah Erdreich
Proofreader: Beth Baumgartel
Book Design and Layout: Judy Morgan
Cover Design: everlution design

Printed in China

This paperback edition published 2010

First published in the United States of America by
Creative Publishing international, Inc., a member of
Quayside Publishing Group
400 First Avenue North
Suite 300
Minneapolis, MN 55401
1-800-328-3895
www.creativepub.com

contents

introduction

*N*eedle felting is my passion and through this book I will share it with you. Most likely, you've dabbled in knitting, sewing, quilting, or even clay or woodworking. The bottom line is you probably like to work with your hands. When I'm doing a public demonstration, I often hear "I don't need another complicated hobby or craft." But needle felting is different! All you need to get started is some wool, a barbed needle, and a foam pad. You will be amazed at what you can create.

There are a few types of felting, with wet felting being the most common form. Wool fibers are separated by hand and placed in layers into the desired pattern. With the addition of hot soapy water and agitation, the result is a felted fabric.

Another popular felting method is to knit with wool yarn and then once the project is completed, the item is thrown into the washing machine with hot soapy water to agitate and felt. Needle felting does not involve wetting the fibers. You simply mold and shape wool with a barbed needle.

I was drawn to needle felting because I wanted more control working with wool and I wanted to make detailed figures and animals in three-dimensional forms. The felting needle was the key to my success. By using this tool, I was able to make all sorts of animals and characters with as much detail as I wanted. I especially enjoy needle felting because it doesn't involve any measuring, weighing, counting, cutting, or other obstacles to creativity. It is a free-form and liberating craft experience!

In this book, I will share some needle-felting techniques that I have developed over the past few years. The goal is to encourage you to try needle felting and explore the many ways you can play with it. Let your imagination soar!

So without further ado, let's get started!

Most of the projects in this book require simple materials. A felting needle, wool, and a foam pad are needed for all projects. Resources for where to find these items are listed on page 128.

materials

The Felting Needle

There are three basic types of industrial felt. Woven felt is wool or a blend of wool and other yarn that is woven into a cloth and then felted using steam and pressure to make the fibers interlock. Pressed felt is the oldest type of fabric known, predating weaving and knitting, and is produced simply by pressing fibers together and steaming to naturally interlock the fibers. The third type of industrial felt, needled felt, is produced by a machine that carries thousands of felting needles and moves up and down to mechanically interlock fibers. The felting needle is a long, sharp, three- or five-sided barbed instrument. Sounds dangerous, eh? This needle is the tool used for sculptural needle felting.

Felting needles come in a variety of gauges from fine (forty gauge) to coarse (thirty-eight gauge) and they vary in the number of sides on the bottom shaft (three to five). The sides of the needle have tiny barbs poking out. Some of the barbs are close together and some are further apart. I recommend starting with a thirty-eight-gauge triangular (three-sided) needle. This size is considered standard.

The projects in this book only require using one needle at a time. There are needle holders available that can hold two to sixteen needles at a time. The needle holders have a handle that unscrews so you can put the needles in and remove them. This tool is good if you want to make a large sculpture or large flat piece of felt.

Store your needle in a safe place when you are not using it. I usually poke my needle deep into the side of a foam pad. Take care not to bend the needles. They are strong but brittle and they will break when bent. It goes without saying, try not to poke yourself while working. Watch your hands while you work.

Foam

You will need to have a piece of foam or sponge to absorb the needle when it penetrates through the wool. The best surface to use for needle felting is high-density foam that is at least 1½" (3.8 cm) thick. Place the wool on the pad and keep needling without worrying about poking your leg or breaking your needle. Some craft stores sell upholstery foam, which can be used in a pinch, but it breaks down faster than the high-density foam.

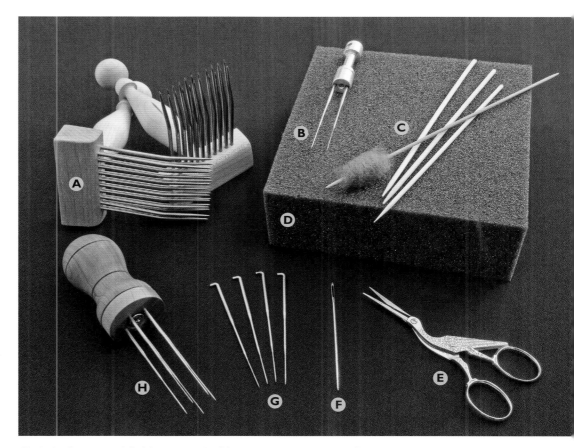

Clockwise from upper left: (A) wool combs, (B) metal two-needle holder, (C) wooden skewers for shaping wool, (D) foam, (E) embroidery scissors, (F) sewing needle for adding details, (G) felting needles (see close-up at left), (H) wooden five-needle holder

Wool

Almost any fiber can be needled—your hair, your kitty's hair, dog hair, mohair, llama, and alpaca fiber. I find that sheep's wool is the absolute best thing to use for needle felting. Why? Because sheep are cute. No, not really. Wool fiber has scales on it. When you poke the felting needle into the wool, the barbs on the sides of the needle make contact with the scales on the wool and cause them to tangle together. In essence, that is felt-making. The more you poke, the more compact the wool fiber becomes. This is where the magic begins . . . .

Some types of wool fibers are better for needle felting than others. This has to do with the coarseness of the wool. Wool types are named for the sheep breed from which they came. In addition, wool fiber that has been overly processed (known as "top") can be a bit more difficult to work with.

Romney wool lends itself well to needle felting. Romney is not too fine, not too coarse. Corriedale is the kind of wool most readily available in spinning stores and is also nice to use. Other wool types that do well for needle felting include Black Welsh Mountain, Border Leicester, Lincoln, Jacob, and Southdown.

Merino is not recommended for needle felting. The fibers are too fine and slippery. Conversely, merino is the best wool to use for wet felting.

Working with Wool Fibers

If you have not yet had the pleasure of working with unspun wool, then you are in for a treat! It's soft and smells sweet—just having a room full of wool is nice. Wool embodies all of the wonderful qualities of natural fibers. It absorbs and reflects light, holds warmth, and is gentle on your hands. And you are using a renewable material! Dyed wool roving is easy to find, thanks to the increasing interest in fiber arts and crafts. Unless the fiber is merino, it should be easy to use for needle felting.

Most of the unspun wool available in stores has already been washed and carded or combed into

○ Different types of unspun sheep's wool.

○ Combed wool. Clockwise from top left: merino, Romney, Southdown, Corriedale.

long ropes or what is called roving. Some wool roving is called top roving, which means that the wool has been combed rather than carded. Fibers felt better if they are laid crosswise rather than in the same direction as with roving. Wool batting is good to use because the fibers have not yet been combed or carded. Batting is coarser than roving, too, which is better for needle felting.

If you really want a hands-on experience, you can start with raw wool. You can find raw wool at local sheep farms or at your local county and state fairs. Washing the wool is easy. Fill a tub with hot water, add a little dish soap, and let the wool soak without agitating it. It is very important not to agitate the wool while it is in the hot water or it may felt. Soak the wool for about an hour, rinse, and repeat. When the rinse water is clean, lay the wool out on towels and roll to absorb the water. Or put the wool in the spin-cycle only of your washing machine. Let the wool dry completely.

Dyeing Wool

There is enough information on dyeing wool and other fibers to write another book. The main thing to keep in mind is that you will probably want to experiment to find out what works best for you. Some fiber artists use only natural dyes from plants. This method involves applying a mordant to the wool so that the dye can be absorbed. Other people use soft-drink mixes and icing color dye. I prefer acid dyes. Acid dyes are made from chemicals and are usually available in a powder form. The acid (white vinegar) is what helps the wool absorb the dye. The dyes come in a large variety of colors, are easy to use, and are cost-effective. As long as the wool absorbs all of the dye in the dye bath, the leftover water is safe for the environment. See the list of resources on page 128 for more information on where to purchase dye. Be sure to follow the manufacturer's safety instructions when using dyes.

○ Dyed, carded wool. Clockwise from top left: blue Corriedale, blue Romney, green Romney, and blended merino.

Sculptural needle felting involves a few easy techniques. Practice each of these processes and you will soon have the skills to create any of the projects in this book.

basic techniques

1. Needling

Hold the felting needle in your hand like a pen or pencil. Poke the needle straight into the wool (**A**). The needle doesn't need to penetrate the surface more than ¼" (6 mm) because the barbs are only on the tip of the needle. Lift and poke with the needle, enough to secure the fibers into place. The more you poke, the tighter the fibers get (**B**).

Don't bend the needle, especially when it's already in the wool. The tip of the needle might break off and be stuck inside of your sculpture. That will turn your wooly critter into an airport security threat! Also don't poke too hard or too much. I know it's tempting, but relax. Third, pay attention to where you are poking with the felting needle and watch your fingers. With some practice, you won't have any trouble at all.

2. Rolling

Most of the needle-felted animal projects in this book start out with a round shape. Take a palm full of wool and tear it into smaller pieces, layering these pieces one on top of the other. When you have a nice pillow of wool, fold the top edge down and the side edges in (**C**). Press and fold. Keep folding and pressing the top down and edges in until you have a nice, compact round shape. Needle all around the surface to hold the wool in place. Roll it around in the palm of your hand like a piece of dough.

3. Flat Shapes

To make wings and ears, begin with a flat shape. Tear a piece of wool into smaller pieces and layer the pieces on the foam like a stack of pancakes **(D)**. Needle the surface. Gently remove the piece of wool from the foam and turn it over. Needle the other side **(E)**. Shape the flat piece by folding the sides in and needling **(F)**.

D

E

F

4. Sculpting

Stone and clay sculpture is often done by starting with a large mass. The artist creates the sculpture by removing material from the start. Sculptural needle felting is different. The sculpture is created by adding to, rather than removing from the material. All of the projects in this book start with a core and pieces are added to the core.

Hold a strip of wool roving in your hand. With your fingertips, gradually pull the layers of wool apart from each other. It is good to start the sculpture process with layers of wool rather than trying to work with a large mass. It is much more difficult to get the wool to behave the way you'd like it to when you start out with too much. Building layers is the way to go.

As you read the projects, you will often see the phrase "keep the fibers loose at one end" after sculpting a body part. It is easier to connect pieces together if the fibers are loose and not already felted. That way, the loose fibers will felt onto the fibers of the body and cre-ate a secure attachment. Adding a bit more wool around the attachment will make it look smooth and natural (see **G–J**).

This may seem confusing now, but don't worry. As you go through the projects, it will make much more sense. Just remember to use layers of wool rather than a large clump to get the best results. And by keeping the fibers loose at one end, the surface area of the attachment place is increased and makes for a more secure attachment.

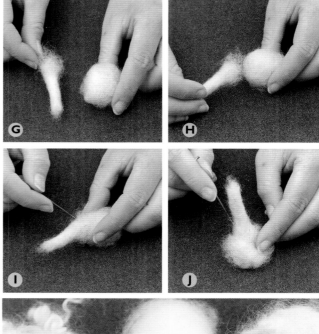

G

H

I

J

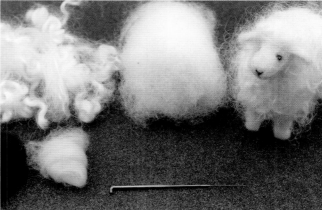

bug magnets

If you are just learning how to needle felt, start with this project. You'll have a charming set of magnets and be encouraged to try making other things. I use a very small rare earth magnet in this project. Be sure not to let pets or children play with the ladybug and bumblebee if you choose to use the same kind of magnet because they are so small and can be a choking hazard.

MATERIALS

- 0.07 oz. (2 g) red wool
- 0.07 oz. (2 g) black wool
- small amount of yellow and white wool
- craft glue
- small rare earth magnet
- beads for eyes
- beading needle and thread
- felting needle
- foam pad
- ruler

BUMBLEBEE

1. Roll a piece of black wool into a 1" (2.5 cm) ball. Needle the surface. This will be the bumblebee's body.

2. Twist a small piece of yellow wool between your fingertips. Lay the stripe around the middle of the bumblebee and needle to attach. Needle two more stripes onto the body, one in front and one behind the middle stripe.

WINGS

3. Fold a piece of white wool into the size and shape of a thumbnail. Needle the surface. Make two.

4. Lay the wings on the back of the bumblebee and needle to attach.

5. On the bottom of the bumblebee's body, place a drop of craft glue and lay the magnet on the glue. Allow the glue to set for a couple of hours.

6. Needle a patch of black wool to cover the magnet. Needle the patch over the magnet and around the bottom of the bumblebee, being careful not to jab the needle into the magnet.

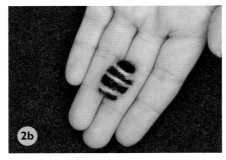

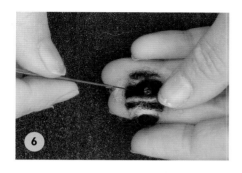

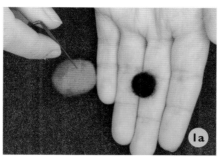

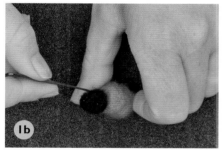

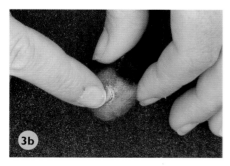

7. Sew black beads onto the front of the bumblebee for eyes.

LADYBUG

1. Roll a piece of red wool into a 1" (2.5 cm) ball for the body. Roll a smaller piece of black wool into a ½" (1.3 cm) ball for the head. Needle the surface of each ball to hold the shape. Attach the head to the body by needling the black ball onto the front of the red ball.

2. Lay a thin strip of black wool down the middle of the ladybug's back. Needle the strip to the body. Roll a few tiny black spots between your fingertips and needle them to the ladybug's back.

3. Put a drop of glue on the bottom of the ladybug's body and place the magnet on the glue.

Allow this to dry for a couple of hours.

4. Needle a 1" (2.5 cm) piece of black wool into a circle that will fit under the ladybug's body. After the glue has set, needle this patch of black wool onto the bottom of the ladybug to cover the magnet.

Be careful not to jab the felting needle into the magnet.

5. Sew black beads onto the head of the ladybug for eyes.

penguin & chick

Penguins have a humorous, clownlike appearance that gives them character. The penguin and chick in this project are easy to make and in a few hours, you can create a whole family.

MATERIALS

- 0.1 oz. (3 g) white wool
- 0.07 oz. (2 g) dark gray wool
- small amount of orange, yellow, and black wool
- black beads for eyes
- beading needle and thread
- wooden skewer
- felting needle
- foam pad
- ruler

PENGUIN BODY

1. Begin the body with a 10" × 2" (25.4 × 5.1 cm) piece of white wool. Roll the wool into a 3½" × 1½" (8.9 × 3.8 cm) sausage shape. Needle the surface smooth.

HEAD

2. Measure a 6" × 2" (15.2 × 5.1 cm) piece of dark gray wool. Roll it into a 1" (2.5 cm) ball and needle the surface smooth.

ATTACHING THE HEAD TO THE BODY

3. Place the head on the top of the body and needle all around the head to connect it to the body.

Turn the body over and needle from the body into the head to make it more secure. Be sure the head is firmly attached to the body before going on to the next step.

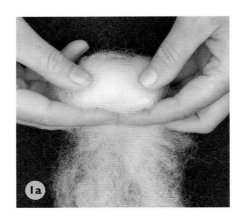

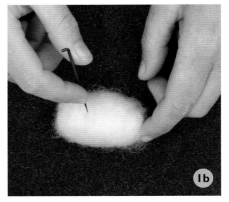

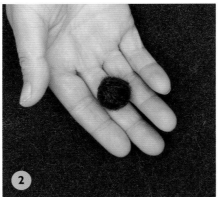

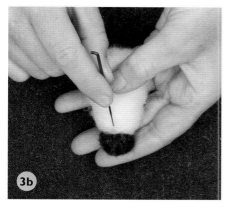

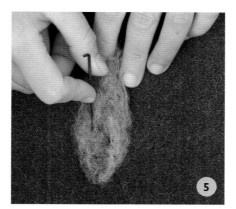

BACK

4. Measure a 10" × 2" (25.4 × 5.1 cm) piece of dark gray wool and divide it into three parts.

5. To make the back, use one of the three pieces of dark gray wool. Needle the wool to flatten and smooth the surface. Shape the piece into a flat oval.

6. Lay the dark gray oval on the back of the body, extending it up to the neck. Needle to attach it to the body.

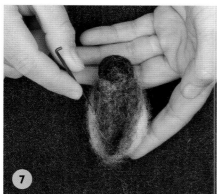

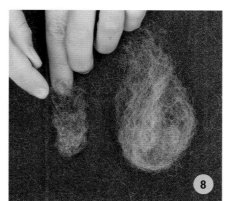

7. Shape the back using the photo as a guide. Needle the dark gray wool on the bottom of the back into a point for the tail. Pull the top of the back around the penguin's neck towards the front on each side, like a collar. It resembles a penguin wearing a cape.

WINGS

The other two pieces of dark gray wool will be used to make the wings.

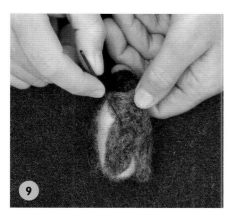

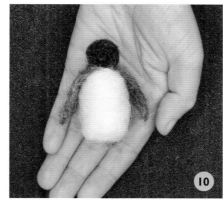

8. Fold one piece of wool in half and needle into a wing shape, about 1½" (3.8 cm) long. Leave the fibers loose at one end for attachment to the body. Shape the wing so that the bottom is pointed.

9. Lay the loose fibers of the wing on the side of the penguin's body and needle to attach. Use the photo as a guide for positioning.

10. Repeat steps 8 and 9 for the other wing.

(continued)

FLIPPERS

11. Fold a 1" (2.5 cm) square piece of black wool into a triangle shape. Needle the shape, keeping the fibers loose at one end for attaching to the body.

12. Needle the loose fibers onto the bottom of the penguin's body.

13. Repeat for the other flipper.

BEAK

14. Wrap a pinch of black wool around a skewer into a cone shape about ½" (1.3 cm) long.

15. Slide the beak off of the skewer and lay it on the penguin's face. Needle the beak to the face around the edges of the beak.

DETAILS

16. Needle a piece of orange wool onto each side of the penguin's head. Add a piece of yellow wool to the top of the penguin's chest. Add a little orange wool to the top of the yellow.

17. Needle a very thin piece of orange wool on either side of the beak.

18. Sew black beads to the face for eyes. Needle a small piece of white wool next to each bead.

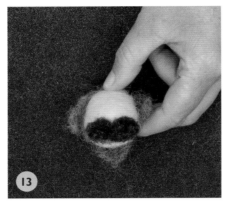

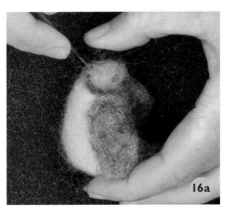

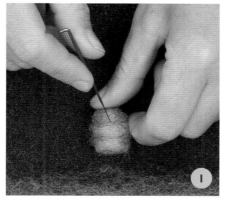

CHICK

The chick can be made with leftover materials from the penguin.

1. Measure a 5" x 2" (12.7 x 5.1 cm) piece of gray wool, roll it into a ½" (1.3 cm)-long sausage and needle it smooth. Needle one end of the sausage shape flat so that the chick can stand.

2. Wrap a small piece of black wool around the top of the sausage shape for a head.

3. Needle two circles of white wool onto the black wool for eyes.

4. Roll a pinch of orange wool around a skewer into a cone shape. Slide it off of the skewer and needle onto the chick's face, between the white eye spots.

5. Fold a piece of black wool into a triangle for flippers. Needle to the bottom of the chick's body.

6. Make wings by folding a piece of gray wool into an oval and needle it to the side of the chick's body. Repeat for the other wing.

7. To complete the eyes, sew black beads onto the white circles.

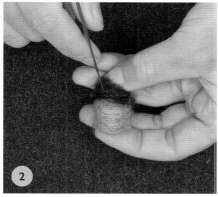

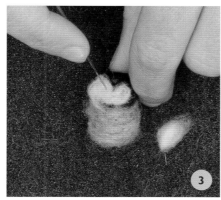

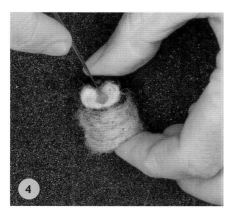

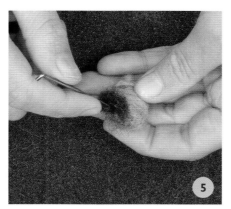

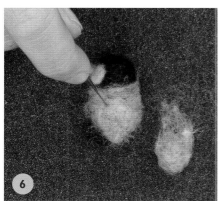

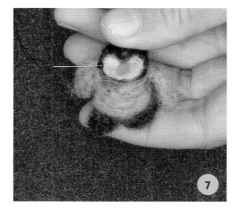

butterfly pin

This is another great project for beginners. Having only simple shapes, this pattern gives you a chance to focus on how to work with wool and the felting needle. You can find blank pin backs in the jewelry-making section of any craft store. Choose the pin back that you can sew on. This pattern makes a 3" (7.6 cm)-wide butterfly.

MATERIALS

- 0.2 (6 g) yellow wool
- small amount of dark brown wool
- pin back
- wooden skewer
- felting needle
- sewing needle and black thread
- foam pad
- ruler

UPPER WINGS

1. Measure a 4" × 2" (10.2 × 5.1 cm) piece of yellow wool. Fold the wool into a triangle with 1½" (3.8 cm)-long sides and needle. Turn the triangle over and needle the other side. Keep the fibers loose at one corner for attaching to the other wing. Make two.

2. Overlap the corners with loose fibers and needle the wings together.

LOWER WINGS

3. Repeat steps 1 and 2, only make the lower wings a little smaller, starting with a 3" × 1" (7.6 × 2.5 cm) piece of yellow wool.

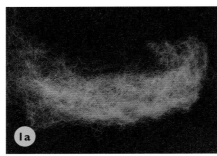
1a

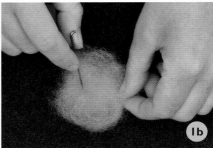
1b

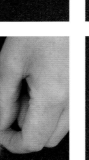

1c

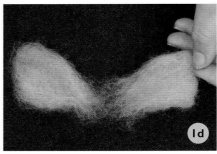
1d

2

3a

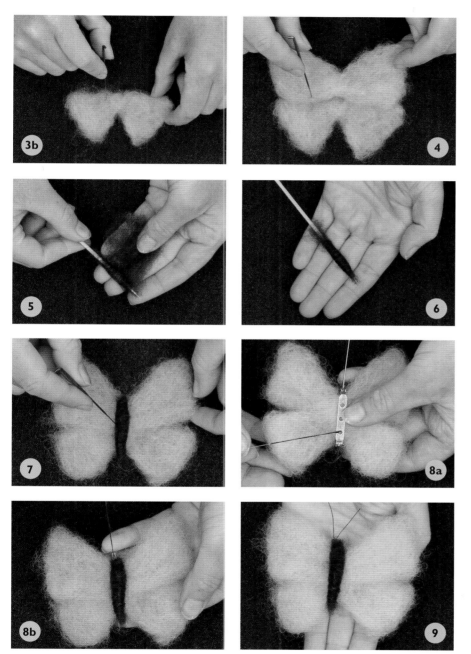

4. Needle the upper wings to the lower set of wings.

BODY

5. Measure a 3" × 1" (7.6 × 2.5 cm) piece of dark brown wool and roll it on the skewer into a 1½" (3.8 cm)-long shape that is about the width of a green bean.

6. Slide the dark brown body off of the skewer and needle the surface.

7. Choose which side of the butterfly will be the front and needle to attach the body between the wings. Needle up and down the body so that it is firmly attached.

8. Turn the butterfly over so that the body is facing down. Lay the pin back between the wings, parallel to the body. Securely sew the pin to the butterfly.

9. With the pin open, needle a small patch of yellow wool over the pin back to cover it. Needle around the pin so that you have a smooth surface. Sew a piece of thread through the head and tie the ends in a knot on the head. Trim to the desired length.

bunny

Hide this palm-size bunny in a basket with some green wool over the top for a springtime gift. The bunny in this project is made with white wool, but you can also use gray, brown, or black wool.

MATERIALS

- 0.2 oz. (6 g) white wool
- small amounts of black and pink wool
- two black seed beads
- sewing needle and black thread
- felting needle
- foam pad or other soft work surface
- ruler
- beading needle and thread

BODY AND HEAD

1. Measure a 10" × 2" (25.4 × 5.1 cm) piece of white wool. Roll into a 2½" (6.4 cm)-long sausage shape. Needle the surface to keep the wool in place and shape the body.

2. Measure a 4" × 2" (10.2 × 5.1 cm) piece of white wool and roll into a 1" (2.5 cm)-long cone shape. Needle the surface to keep the wool fibers in place and shape the head. Keep the fibers loose at the wider end of the head to help attach it to the body.

3. Needle the loose fibers of the head to the body. Turn the bunny upside down and needle from the bottom of the body up through the head. Add more wool around the neck and needle to smooth the space between the head and body.

EARS

4. Fold a thin strip of white wool in half. Pinch the fibers together at the loose end, but don't needle them. Each ear is 1" (2.5 cm) long. To give the ear a

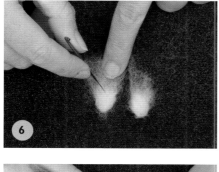

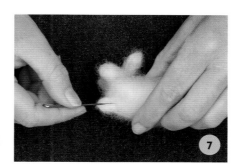

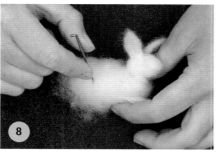

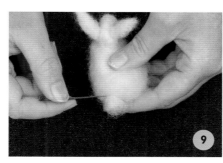

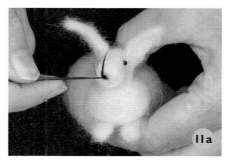

natural curved shape, needle from the edge of the ear towards the middle. Make two ears.

5. Attach the ears to the head by needling the loose fibers at the base of the ears. Needle deeper at the inside bottom of the ear.

FRONT PAWS

6. Needle a piece of white wool that is about the size of a thumbnail into an oval shape. Leave the fibers loose at one end for attaching the paw to the body. Make two.

7. Position the front paws to the underside of the body. Needle the loose fibers of the paws onto the body to attach them.

8. Add a little extra wool to the back end of the body.

9. To make the tail, needle a small tuft of white wool to the back of the bunny.

10. Sew a black bead on each side of the head for eyes.

11. Needle a thin strip of black wool down the middle of the bunny's snout. Split the fibers above the line into a Y shape and needle. Cut off any excess wool. Split the fibers on the bottom of the line into an upside-down Y shape and needle. Cut off any excess wool.

12. Needle a pinch of pink wool on the inside of the bunny's ear. Repeat on the other ear.

owl

This pattern makes a 3" (7.6 cm)-tall brown owl with talons made from wire. Use all-white wool instead of gray wool to make a snowy owl.

MATERIALS

- 0.3 oz. (9 g) gray wool
- small amount of white, dark brown, yellow, and black merino wool
- 6" (15.2 cm) piece of 24-gauge wire, preferably black
- needle-nose pliers
- 1 yd. (91.4 m) gold embroidery floss
- felting needle
- foam pad or other soft work surface
- ruler
- wooden skewer

BODY

1. Measure an 8" × 3" (20.3 × 7.6 cm) piece of gray wool.

2. Roll tightly into a 2½" (6.4 cm)-long barrel shape. Needle the surface to keep the fibers from unrolling and to create a firm, smooth surface.

HEAD

3. Measure a 7" × 2" (17.8 × 5.1 cm) piece of gray wool.

4. Roll tightly into a 1½" (3.8 cm)-long barrel shape. Needle the surface all around the head to help hold the shape.

5. Attach the head to the body by laying the barrel-shaped head on its side and needling it to the top of the body. Needle all around the edge of the head to attach.

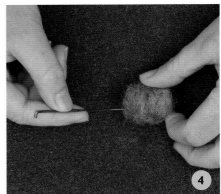

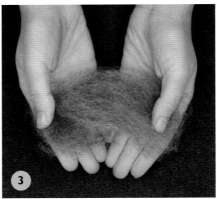

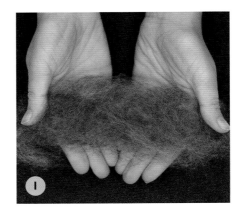

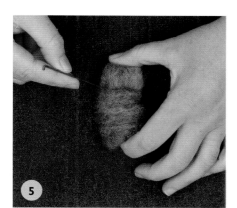

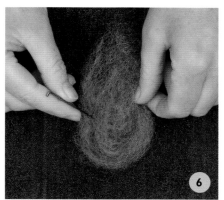

WINGS

6. Measure a 6" × 2" (15.2 × 5.1 cm) piece of brown wool and divide in half.

7. Fold one of the brown pieces of wool so that it measures 1½" (3.8 cm) long and needle the surface flat. Form the wing shape by folding the fibers into a point at one end and needling them in place. Leave the fibers at the other end loose for attaching the wing to the body.

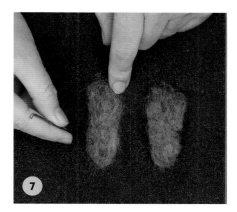

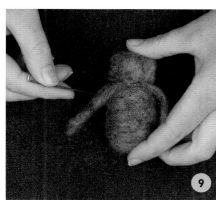

8. Lay the loose fibers of the wing on the side of the owl's body and needle to attach. Use the photo as a guide for positioning.

9. Repeat steps 7 and 8 for the other wing.

TAIL

10. Fold a 2" (5.1 cm)-long piece of brown wool into a triangle shape. Keep the fibers loose at one end for attaching the tail to the body.

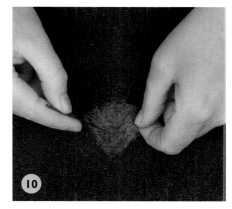

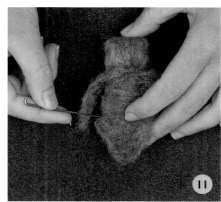

11. Needle the loose fibers of the tail to the back end of the body. The tail should extend about ¼" (6 mm) below the body.

(continued)

12. Add a layer of white wool to the owl's chest.

EYES

13. Fold two pieces of dark brown wool into flat oval shapes. Needle these shapes onto each side of the owl's face. Leave a space for the beak in between.

14. Needle a smaller piece of yellow wool on the dark brown wool and needle an even smaller piece of black wool on the yellow wool. Add a white speck on the middle of the black wool.

BEAK

15. Roll a pinch of yellow wool around the tip of the skewer into a cone shape. Slide the yellow wool off of the skewer and needle to keep the wool in place.

16. Position the beak in the middle of the owl's face between the eyes. Needle the beak to the face and pull the pointed end forward and slightly down.

FACIAL DETAILS

17. Add a strip of white wool above each of the owl's eyes and needle to attach.

18. Lay a strip of white wool under the owl's eyes and needle to attach.

EARS

19. Fold a dime-sized piece of gray wool into a triangle and needle the surface. Leave the fibers loose at one end to attach the ear to the head. Make a second ear.

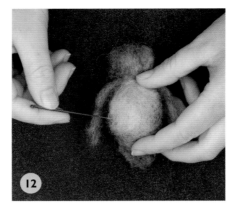

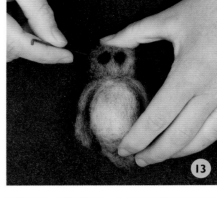

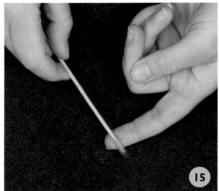

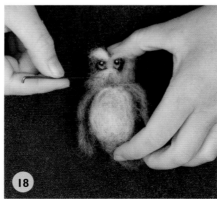

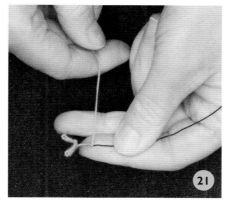

20. Position the ear on top of the side of the owl's head and needle the loose fibers to attach. Needle deeper in the inner ear to help create a curved look.

TALONS

21. Tightly wrap the gold embroidery floss around the wire.

22. On one end, begin to shape the talons by bending the wire, using the needle nose pliers, into four ¼" (6 mm)-long U shapes. Squeeze the U's together to make a talon. To make the back talon, use the pliers to turn the last front talon around to the back.

23. Repeat on the other end of the wire for the other talons.

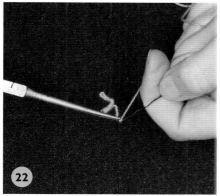

ATTACHING THE TALONS TO THE BODY

24. Shape the wire so that the talons are both facing forward and the wire in between them is in an arc shape. Wrap a few layers of brown wool around the middle of the wire legs and lay the wool-wrapped wire on the bottom of the owl's body.

25. Needle the brown wool-wrapped legs onto the body. Be careful to avoid jabbing the felting needle into the wire.

26. Adjust the talons so that the owl can stand.

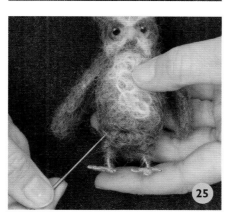

goldfinch

This pattern is for a goldfinch, but you can make other backyard birds by changing the color of the wool. The goldfinch measures 3" (7.6 cm) including the tail.

MATERIALS

- 0.1 oz. (3 g) golden-yellow wool
- small amount of black, orange, and white wool
- black beads for eyes
- sewing needle and thread
- felting needle
- foam pad
- wooden skewer
- ruler
- 6" (15.2 cm) piece of ribbon to hang the bird

BODY

1. Measure a 7" × 2" (17.8 × 5.1 cm) piece of golden-yellow wool.

2. Roll tightly and shape it into a 2" (5.1 cm)-long oblong shape that is wide at one end and narrow at the other. Needle the body to keep it from unrolling.

3. Needle the tail end flat. Shape the head end by adding more wool and needling it smooth and rounded.

WINGS

4. Fold a 1" (2.5 cm) piece of black wool in half. Use the photo as a guide for how to shape the wing. The shoulder end of the wing is rounded and the opposite end comes to a point. Make two wings.

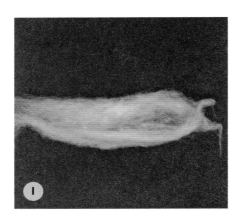

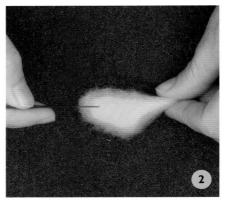

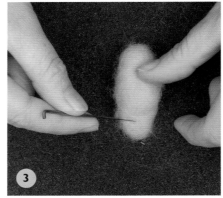

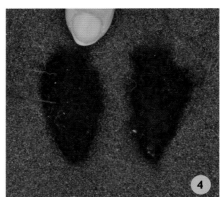

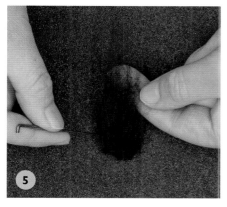

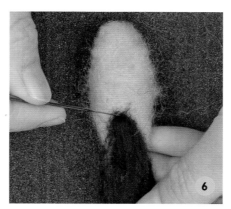

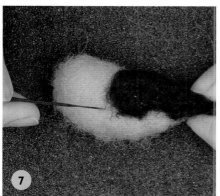

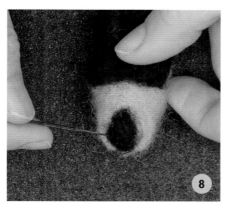

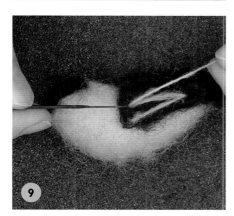

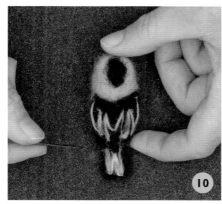

TAIL

5. Fold a 1" (2.5 cm) piece of black wool into a long rectangle. Needle the tail shape flat, turn it over and needle the other side. Leave the fibers loose at one end for attaching the tail to the body.

ATTACHING THE TAIL AND WINGS TO THE BODY

6. Lay the loose fibers on the tail onto the back end of the bird's body. The tail should extend out past the end of the body by ¾" (1.9 cm). Needle the loose fibers to attach the tail.

7. Position the wings on the upper back part of the bird. Needle the wings to the bird.

8. Needle a flat, dime-sized piece of black wool onto the goldfinch's forehead.

FEATHER DETAILS

9. Twist some white wool between your fingers until it becomes a long thread. Lay the thread on the wing and needle it down to secure. Make a feather pattern by laying the wool thread down then needling it in place, going back and forth along the side of the wing.

10. Repeat for the other wing and add detail to the tail.

(continued)

11. Roll a piece of orange wool on the end of the skewer to make a cone-shaped beak. Needle the beak to the front of the bird's face, below the black cap.

12. Sew black beads onto each side of the head for eyes.

13. Thread a piece of ribbon through the center of the bird's body, make a loop, and tie a knot on the underside of the body to secure the ribbon.

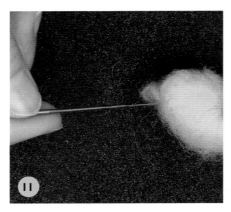

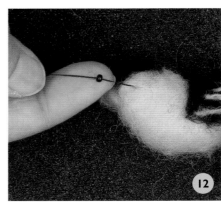

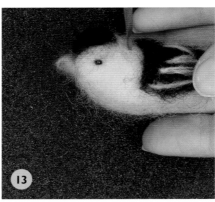

VARIATIONS

Chickadee

Use the same proportions as the goldfinch, but make the body using white wool. The wings and tail are black. In addition to a black cap, the chickadee has a black chin. Add gold to the chickadee's breast.

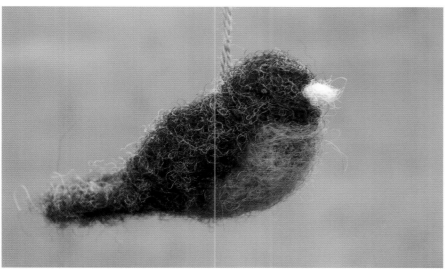

Robin

Make the body using gray-brown wool. Give the robin a rosy breast. Robin's heads are smaller in proportion to the rest of their body.

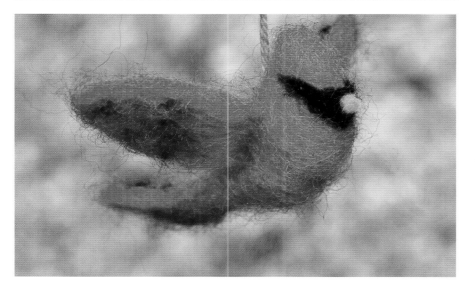

Cardinal

Use red for the body, wings, and tail. Cardinals have an orange beak and black mask. They also have a red crest. Use gray or black wool for feather details.

turtle

Slow and steady wins the race. This applies to needle-felting too! As you make the turtle, take your time and enjoy the process. This pattern makes a 3" (7.6 cm)-long green turtle, just the right size for the palm of your hand.

MATERIALS

- 0.2 oz. (6 g) green wool
- small amount of dark green and black wool
- black beads for eyes
- sewing needle and thread
- felting needle
- foam pad or other soft work surface
- wooden skewer
- ruler

BODY

1. Measure a 10" × 2" (25.4 × 5.1 cm) piece of green wool for the body.

2. Fold the wool into a 2" × 1½" (5.1 × 3.8 cm) flat oval shape. Needle to flatten and shape the surface.

HEAD

3. Measure a 3" × 1" (7.6 × 2.5 cm) piece of green wool.

4. Roll tightly into a 1" (2.5 cm) ball. Needle the surface to keep the fibers in place. Leave the fibers loose at one end for attaching the head to the body.

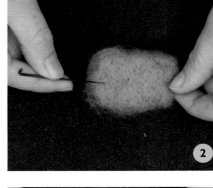

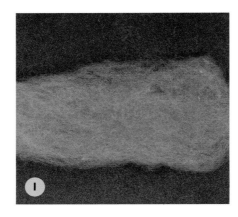

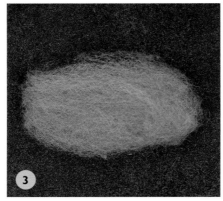

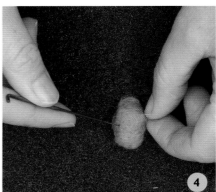

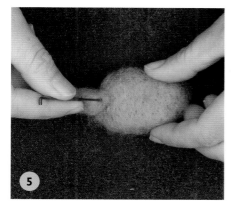

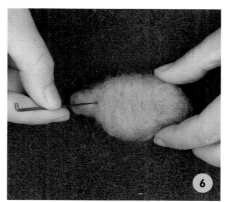

ATTACHING THE HEAD TO THE BODY

5. Lay the loose fibers of the head piece onto the top of the body and needle to attach.

6. Turn the body over and needle it from underneath.

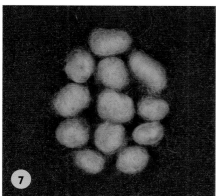

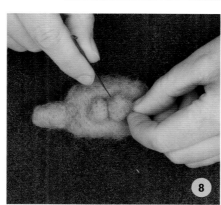

SHELL

7. To make the sections on the turtle shell, roll twelve small balls of green wool. The balls should have a diameter of about ½" (1.3 cm).

8. Start at the center of the turtle's body and needle each green section onto the body.

9. Cover the entire shell.

10. Use dark green wool to needle a swirl onto the top of each section.

(continued)

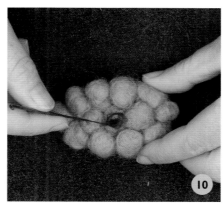

11. Needle a dark green outline in between the sections of the shell.

LEGS

12. Roll a 3" × 2" (7.6 × 5.1 cm) piece of green wool around a wooden skewer into a 1½" (3.8 cm)-long tube shape. Keep the fibers loose at one end for attaching the leg to the body.

13. On the opposite end of the leg, needle the fibers from the outside edge in to make a foot. Needle the foot flat on the bottom. Make three more legs the same way.

ATTACHING THE LEGS TO THE BODY

14. Position the legs on the turtle's body and needle the loose fibers from underneath. Turn the turtle over and needle from the top down.

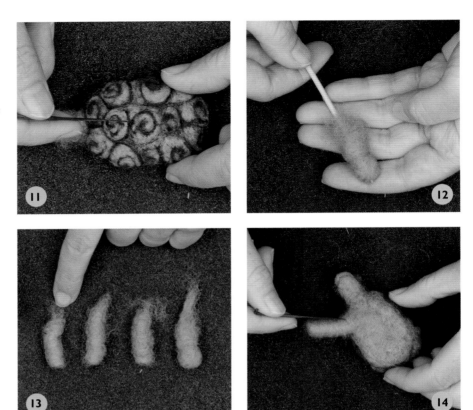

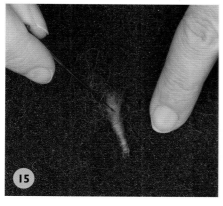

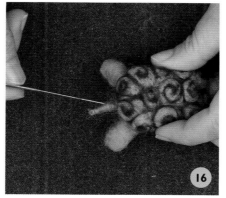

TAIL

15. Roll a small piece of green wool into a cone shape using the end of a wooden skewer. Slide the tail off of the skewer and needle to keep the fibers in place.

16. Attach the tail to the turtle's back.

EYES AND MOUTH

17. Sew black beads onto the side of the turtle's head for eyes.

18. Needle a thin piece of black wool onto the turtle's face for a mouth.

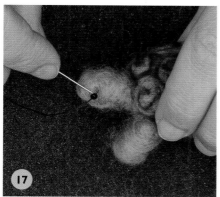

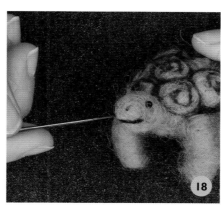

bat

If you like decorating for Halloween, you'll enjoy this project. The bats are easy to make, so make a bunch of them! Hang the bats from a bare tree branch to make a spooky bat mobile.

MATERIALS

FOR ONE BAT

- 0.1 oz. (3 g) black wool
- beading needle and thread
- black beads for eyes
- felting needle
- foam pad
- ruler

THE WINGS

1. Measure a 7" × 2" (17.8 × 5.1 cm) piece of black wool. Needle the surface of the piece of wool so that it is flat and smooth. Turn the piece over and needle the other side.

2. Fold in the sides and needle to shape into a triangle.

3. Using the photo as a guide, needle and shape the bottom of the bat's wings into a scalloped edge. Turn the wings over and needle the other side to help define the edge.

4. Define the top edge of the wings by folding and needling. Pull the middle of the top edge down and needle. It should look like the bat has shoulders. The head will go in this low spot between the shoulders. Check the wings for any thin spots and add more wool if necessary. They should be opaque.

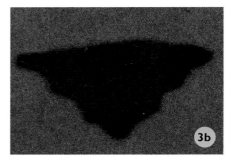

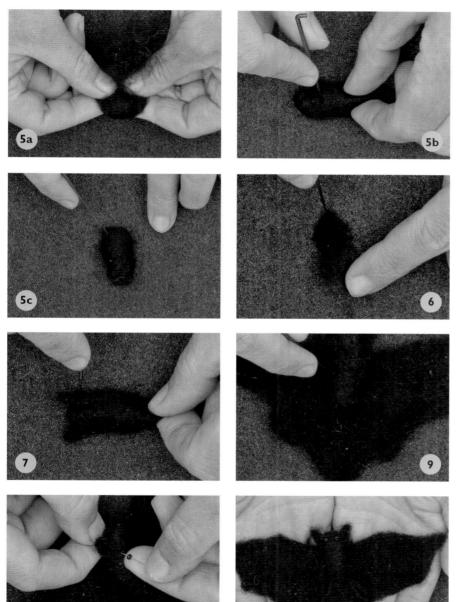

BODY

5. Measure a 4" × 2" (10.2 × 5.1 cm) piece of black wool. Roll it into a sausage shape and needle the surface until the body measures about 1" × ½" (2.5 × 1.3 cm). The body shape should be tapered at the end.

EARS

6. Take a dime-sized piece of black wool and fold it in half. Needle the surface and keep the fibers loose at the flat end for attaching to the bat. Make two ears.

7. Lay the ear on the top side of the body piece. Needle the loose fibers to the head. The ear should stick out above the head. Pinch the top of the bat's ear into a point. Needle to define the pointy ear.

8. Repeat with the other ear.

ATTACHING THE BODY TO THE WINGS

9. Lay the body on the middle of the wingspan. The head should extend above the wings. Needle the body to the wings. Needle around the edge of the body, then turn the bat over and needle through the back of the wings into the body.

10. Sew black beads onto the bat's face for eyes.

chicken & chick

The chicken and chick are easy to make. In the springtime, they can be hidden inside a plastic egg. This pattern makes a 2½" (6.4 cm) chicken and a 1" (2.5 cm) chick.

MATERIALS

- 0.07 oz. (2 g) red-brown wool
- small amount of yellow, red, brown, and black wool
- black beads for eyes
- sewing needle and thread
- felting needle
- foam pad
- wooden skewer
- ruler

CHICKEN BODY

1. Measure a 6" × 3" (15.2 × 7.6 cm) piece of red-brown wool.

2. Roll tightly into a triangle shape. The top part of the triangle measures 2½" (6.4 cm) and will be the chicken's back and tail. The two shorter sides measure 1½" (3.8 cm) and will be the chicken's breast and the underside of the tail. Needle the chicken's body to keep the shape from unrolling.

HEAD

3. Roll a ½" (1.3 cm) ball of red-brown wool and needle to hold the shape.

4. Position the head on the body and needle to attach.

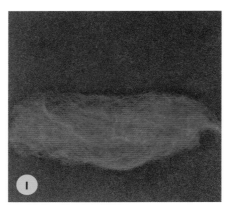

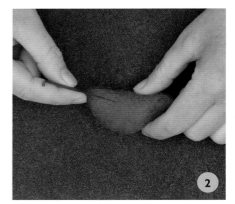

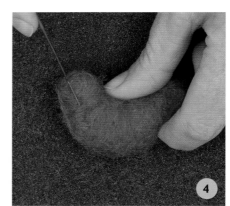

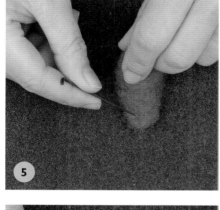

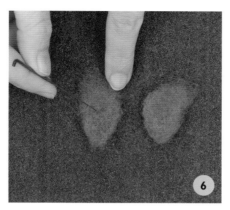

5. Needle the tail into a flat, fan shape. Turn the chicken over and needle the underside of the tail.

WINGS

6. Needle a 1" (2.5 cm)-long piece of red-brown wool into a flat, small wing shape. Make two.

7. Position the wings on either side of the body and needle around the edge of the wings into the body to attach.

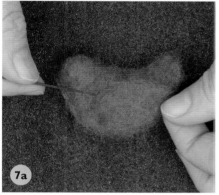

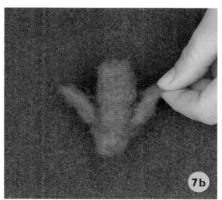

COMB AND BEAK

8. Roll a small piece of red wool between your fingertips and place it on top of the chicken's head. Needle the comb to the chicken's head.

9. Make a cone-shaped beak by rolling a piece of yellow wool on the pointed end of a wooden skewer. Remove the yellow cone from the skewer and needle it onto the chicken's face below the comb.

(continued)

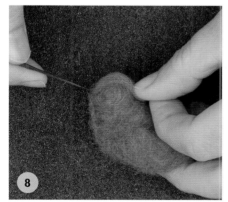

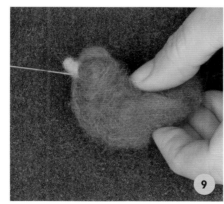

10. Add a piece of red wool to each side of the beak for a waddle.

11. Sew black beads onto the side of the chicken's head for eyes.

CHICK

12. Roll a 3" (7.6 cm)-long piece of yellow wool into a triangle shape that measures 1" (2.5 cm) long. Needle the surface to keep the wool from unrolling.

WINGS

13. Fold a piece of yellow wool into a wing shape. Make two and needle the surface of each wing to shape them.

14. Attach the wings to each side of the chick's body.

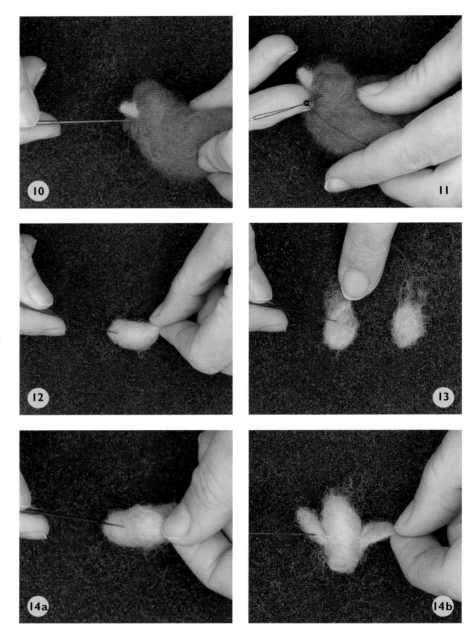

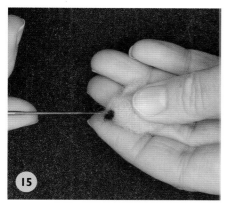

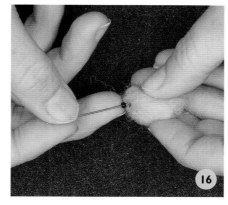

15. Roll a piece of black wool between your fingers and needle it onto the chick's face for a beak.

16. Sew black beads onto each side of the chick's head for eyes.

NEST

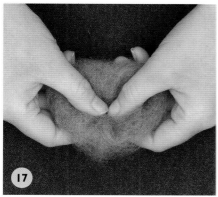

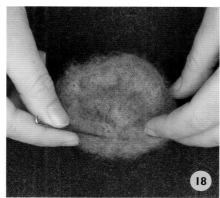

17. Shape a palm-sized amount of brown wool into a bowl shape. Needle the bottom of the nest, then turn it upside down and needle from the opposite side.

18. Lay the nest on its side and needle the sides all around.

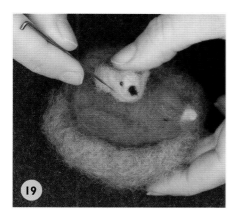

19. Place the chicken and chick inside the nest. If desired, attach the chicken to the nest by needling the fibers at the base of the chicken's body into the base of the nest. The same can be done to attach the chick to the chicken. Position the chick on the back of the chicken and needle the yellow fibers on the bottom of the chick into the chicken's back.

hummingbird

Blending orange wool fibers with copper Angelina fibers will give this felted hummingbird an iridescent glow. Angelina is a fine, synthetic fiber that looks metallic and is easy to blend with wool fiber. The colors in this project are for a rufous hummingbird. Change the colors to green wool and green Angelina fibers to make a ruby-throated or Anna's hummingbird.

MATERIALS

- 0.1 oz. (3 g) orange wool
- small amount of red, white, and black wool
- small amount of copper or red Angelina fiber
- 6" (15.2 cm) piece of ribbon
- acrylic floor shield

- black beads for eyes
- wooden skewer
- felting and darning needles
- foam pad
- ruler
- sewing needle and thread

1. Layer the wool and Angelina fiber and pull gently with your fingers to blend. Layer and pull until the fibers seem well blended. Use this wool for the body, wings, and tail of the hummingbird.

BODY

2. Measure a 4" × 2" (10.2 × 5.1 cm) piece of orange wool. Roll this piece and as you roll, shape it so that one end is the narrow tail and the other end is the wider head. The middle should be the widest part of the roll.

3. Needle the surface to shape it and make it smooth.

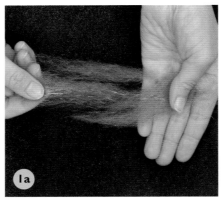

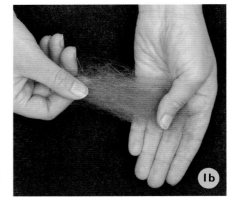

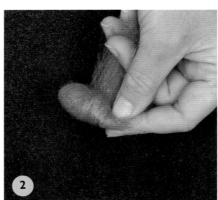

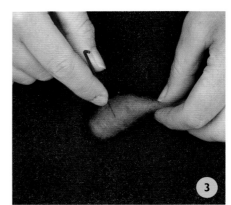

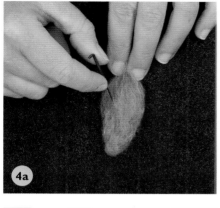

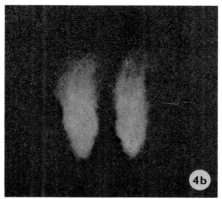

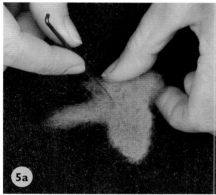

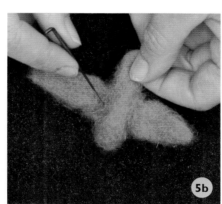

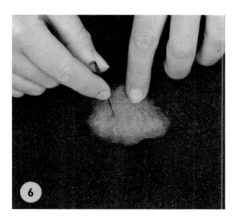

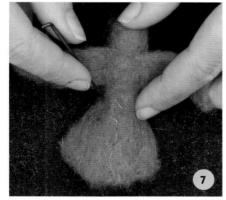

WINGS

4. Measure a 2" × 1" (5.1 × 2.5 cm) piece of orange wool. Fold this piece into a wing shape and needle. Turn the wing over and needle the other side. At the wider end, leave the fibers loose for attaching to the body. Repeat with the other wing.

5. Lay the loose fibers of the wing on the side of the hummingbird's body. The wing should be perpendicular to the body. Needle the loose fibers of the wing onto the body.

Repeat with the other wing. Check to see if the wings are positioned correctly and adjust them if necessary. The wings can easily be removed, repositioned, and needled on again.

TAIL

6. Using the same amount of wool as for a wing, fold the wool into a fan shape with loose fibers at the narrow end for attaching the tail to the body. Needle both sides of the fan-shaped tail.

7. Lay the loose fibers of the tail onto the narrow end of the bird's back and needle to attach. Turn the body over and needle the attachment.

(continued)

BREAST, THROAT, AND BEAK

8. Lay a dime-size piece of white wool on the hummingbird's breast. Needle to attach.

9. Use your fingers to blend a pinch of red wool with a pinch of red or copper Angelina fiber.

10. Lay the blended red wool on the hummingbird's throat and needle.

11. Roll a thin piece of black wool around the wooden skewer. Pull the wool off and twist it between your fingertips.

12. Thread the black wool piece through a darning needle. Pull the needle and the wool from the back of the hummingbird's head to the front, exiting where the beak will be. Don't pull the wool all the way through the head. Leave the tail end of the black wool on the back of the bird's head.

13. Cut and needle the black wool on the back of the bird's head to secure the beak. Cover the spot with a piece of orange wool and needle to blend.

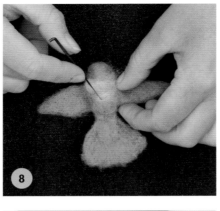

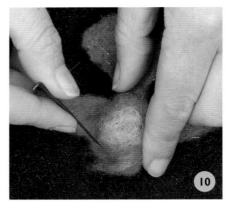

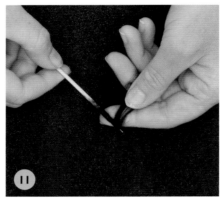

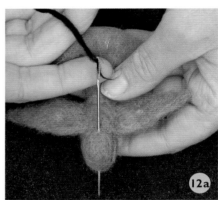

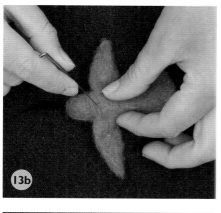

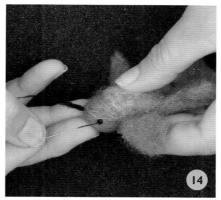

14. Sew black beads onto each side of the hummingbird's head for eyes.

15. To stiffen the beak, dip it in a bottle of acrylic floor shield and let dry.

16. Thread a piece of ribbon through the bird so it can be hung.

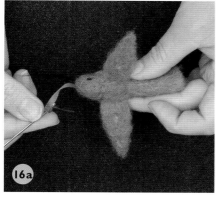

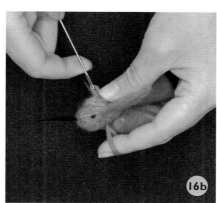

clownfish

Clownfish seem delightful, perhaps because of the bright colors and patterns on their bodies. Hanging the fish from a piece of monofilament will make it appear to swim through the air. Merino wool is recommended for its black and white stripes because of merino's ease of use for needle-felting details. This project will make a 3" (7.6 cm)-long clownfish.

MATERIALS

- 0.2 oz. (6 g) orange wool
- small amount of white and black merino wool
- black beads for eyes
- beading needle and thread
- felting needle
- foam pad
- ruler

BODY

1. Measure a 6" × 2" (15.2 × 5.1 cm) piece of orange wool and fold it into a 2½" (6.4 cm)-long football shape. Needle the surface.

TAIL

2. Fold a 1" (2.5 cm) piece of orange wool into a triangle shape. Leave the fibers loose at one end for attaching the tail to the body.

3. Lay the loose fibers of the tail onto the end of the body and needle to attach.

FINS

4. Fold a small piece of orange wool into the size and shape of a thumbnail. Needle the shape and keep the fibers loose at one end for attaching the fins to the fish's body. Make six fins.

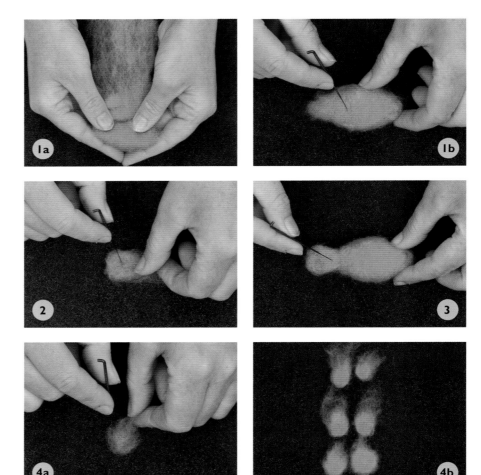

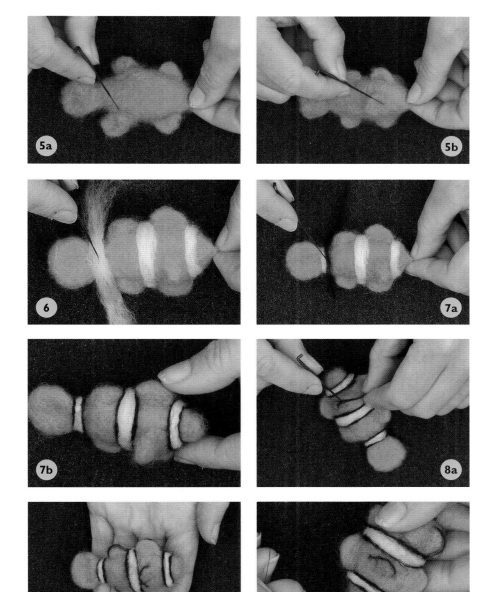

5. Attach two fins to the top of the clownfish, two to the bottom, and one on each side. Use the photos at left as a guide.

STRIPES

6. Lay a thin stripe of white merino wool around the middle of the clownfish body, between the fins. Needle to attach. Lay another stripe of white merino wool around the front of the clownfish, on the face. Needle to attach. Lay a third stripe of white merino wool around the clownfish where the tail and body connect. Needle to attach.

7. Lay a very thin black stripe of merino wool on the outside edge of each white stripe. Needle to attach.

8. Lay a thin black stripe of merino wool on the top edge of each of the six fins. Needle to attach.

9. Sew black beads onto each side of the clownfish face, just in front of the white stripes, for eyes.

chipmunk

When designing this project, picture a chipmunk sitting back on his hind legs with an acorn between his front paws. The basic shape can be used in a variety of positions. Make a squirrel by substituting gray or red-brown wool for brown wool and giving him a bushy tail. This pattern makes a 3" (7.6 cm)-tall chipmunk.

MATERIALS

- 0.3 oz. (9 g) brown wool
- small amount of white and dark brown wool for details
- black beads for eyes
- felting needle
- foam pad
- wooden skewer
- ruler

BODY

The instructions for this animal may seem different for the body as compared to other animals in the book. The chipmunk in this project has a rounded, concave figure. I will explain how you can get the same effect. Use the photos as a guide.

1. Roll an 8" × 2" (20.3 × 5.1 cm) piece of brown wool into a crescent shape. To do this easily, pinch and pull the ends down as the wool is rolled. The roll should be 2½" (6.4 cm) long. Needle the surface. Needle more densely at the area where the roll curves in.

HEAD

2. Roll a 5" × 2" (12.7 × 5.1 cm) piece of brown wool into a cone shape. You can roll the wool around the skewer if it helps you to keep the narrow end pointed. Leave the fibers on the back of the head loose for attaching to the body.

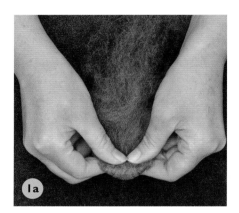

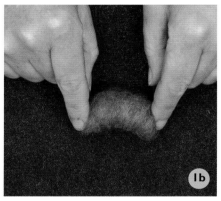

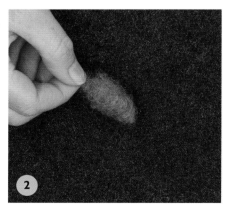

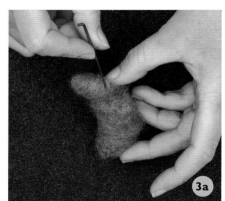

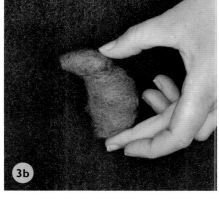

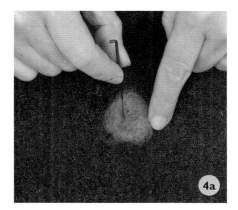

3. Position the head on top of the body and hold it in place with one hand. Needle around the edge of the head where it connects to the body. Turn the chipmunk over and needle from the neck part of the body into the head to form a secure attachment.

HIND LEGS AND PAWS

4. Needle a 1" (2.5 cm) piece of wool into a circle. Lay the circle on the bottom side of the chipmunk's body where the thigh should be. Needle around the thigh to secure.

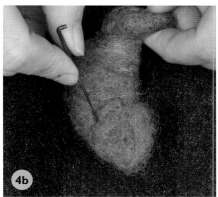

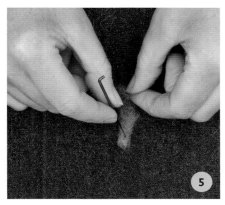

5. The paw is made by needling a thumbnail-sized piece of wool into a curved shape, leaving the fibers loose at one end for attaching to the thigh.

6. Turn the chipmunk over and needle the loose fibers of the paw onto the bottom of the thigh.

7. Repeat steps 4 through 6 with the other hind leg and paw.

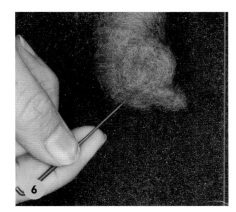

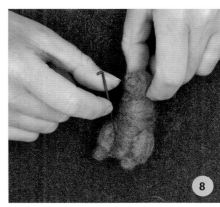

8. Needle at the inner thighs and around to shape the hind legs.

(continued)

FRONT PAWS

9. Roll a 1" (2.5 cm) piece of brown wool on the skewer into a cone shape. Remove the cone from the skewer, needle and keep the fibers loose at the wider end for attaching to the body.

10. Lay the loose fibers of the paws on the side of the chipmunk's body, above the thigh. Needle the paw to the body, keeping the end of the paw unattached.

11. Repeat with the other paw.

EARS

12. Fold a ½" (1.3 cm) piece of brown wool into a triangle. Needle the triangle and keep the fibers loose at one end for attaching the ear to the head. Make two.

13. Lay the loose fibers of the ear on the side of the chipmunk's head. Needle to attach. Needle the inner ear so that the ear is slightly curved. Pinch the end of the ear and twist the wool into a point.

14. Repeat with the other ear.

STRIPES

15. Lay a thin stripe of white wool down the center of the chipmunk's back. Needle the stripe to attach. Lay two thin stripes of dark brown wool on each side of the white stripe and needle to attach. Add two more white stripes to the outside of the dark brown wool and needle.

16. The chipmunk has some stripes on the side of his face. Lay one stripe in the middle of the face, going through the eye line. Needle to attach. Lay two white stripes above and below the dark brown and then two more dark brown stripes

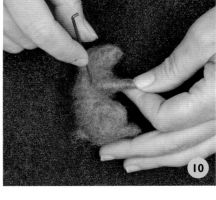
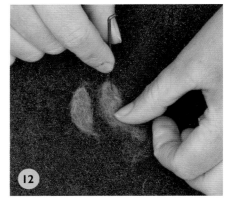
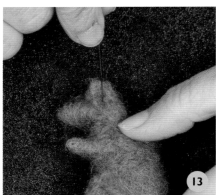
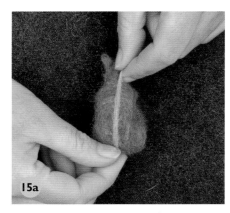

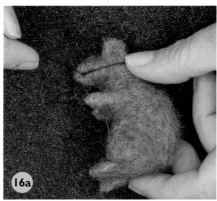
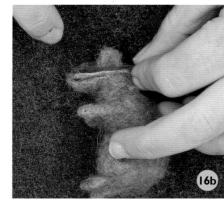

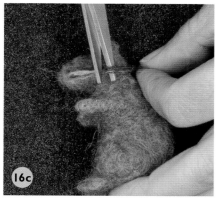

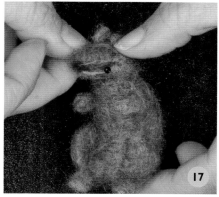

on each side of the white ones. Needle to attach. Use the photo as a guide.

17. Sew a black bead in the middle of the center dark brown stripe for an eye. Repeat on the other side.

18. Roll a piece of dark brown wool into a ball and needle it onto the chipmunk's nose.

TAIL

19. Take a strip of brown wool about 3" (7.6 cm) long, fold it in half lengthwise and needle the surface to shape the tail. Leave the fibers loose at one end. Needle the loose fibers to the bottom of the body to attach the tail.

20. Add a little white wool to the chipmunk's chest and tummy.

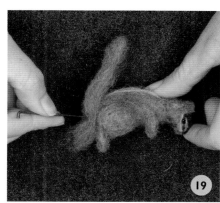

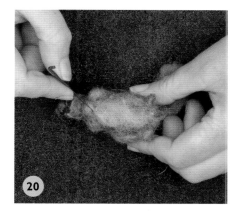

border collie

This pattern is for a specific breed of dog, the border collie. It is easy to modify the color and size of the pattern to create other types of dogs. Use all-black wool instead of black and white to make a Labrador retriever or add curly wool locks to make the dog look like a poodle. If you want to make a Jack Russell terrier, adjust the size of the pattern and make the pieces smaller. This pattern makes a 3½" (8.9 cm)-tall border collie.

MATERIALS

- 0.4 oz. (11 g) white wool
- 0.2 oz. (6 g) black wool
- black beads for eyes
- sewing needle and black thread
- felting needle
- foam pad or other soft work surface
- wooden skewer
- ruler

BODY, HEAD, AND NECK

1. Measure a 7" × 2" (17.8 × 5.1 cm) piece of white wool.

2. Roll it tightly into a 2½" × 1½" (6.4 × 3.8 cm) sausage shape. Needle all over the surface to help form the shape.

3. Measure a 5" × 1" (12.7 × 2.5 cm) piece of white wool.

4. Roll it tightly into a 1" (2.5 cm)-long cone shape. Needle the surface. The fibers should be loose at the wider end of the cone for attaching the head to the body.

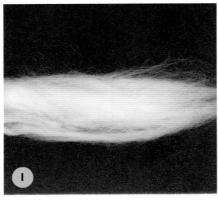

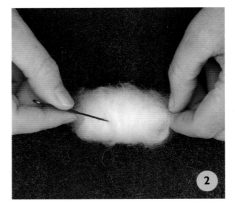

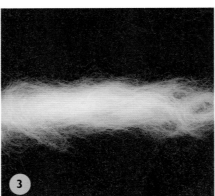

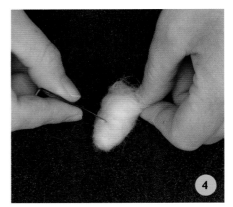

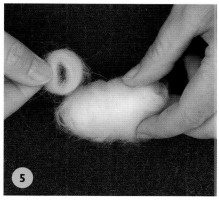

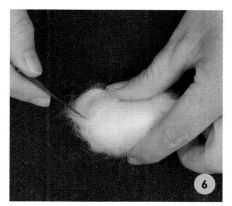

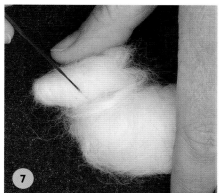

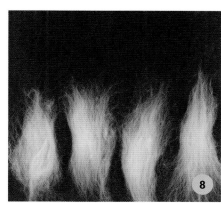

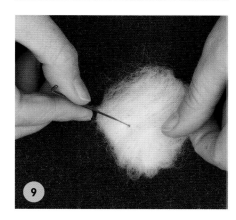

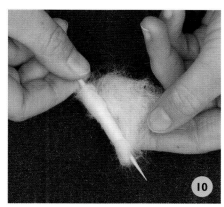

5. Wrap a wisp of white wool around your finger.

6. Place the wisp on top of the body and needle. This piece is the neck and will help fill the space between the head and the body.

7. Attach the head to the body by needling the loose fibers of the head through the neck and into the body. Needle around the edge of the head to attach.

Note: Most of the body, head, and neck area will be covered with a layer of black wool so at this point in the project, it isn't important to get a finished look.

LEGS

8. Measure a 7" × 2" (17.8 × 5.1 cm) piece of white wool and divide it into four equal parts. These will be the legs.

9. Take one of the four pieces of wool and needle the surface flat. Turn the piece over and needle the other side.

10. Roll the flat piece of wool tightly around the skewer. Remove the leg from the skewer and needle to keep it from unrolling. Keep the fibers loose at one end to attach the leg to the body.

(continued)

11. Needle the fibers at the foot end from the edge to the center. Repeat for the other three legs.

ATTACHING THE LEGS TO THE BODY

12. Starting with a back leg, lay the leg halfway up the rear of the body and needle the fibers to attach. Turn the dog's body over and needle the leg at the inner thigh. Add more wool around the area of attachment to help secure the leg in place.

13. Repeat for the other three legs.

ADDING THE BLACK FURRY COAT

14. Tear a ½" (1.3 cm)-long piece of black wool, lay it on the side of the dog near the ribcage, and needle to attach. Needle only the top of the black wool into the body and leave the rest of the fibers loose.

15. Add more black wool to the dog's body as in step 14. Needle one small piece of black wool at a time rather than covering the whole body at once. Add the wool from the bottom side of the body up to the middle of the dog's back, then up the other side of the dog's body to the back, then along the back toward the rear of the dog. Leave the tummy, neck, legs, and head white.

16. Needle a small amount of black wool onto the dog's face on either side of the snout. Leave a white space that runs from the nose, between the eyes, and up to the forehead.

17. Needle a small amount of black wool onto the top of the dog's head and on the sides where the ears will be.

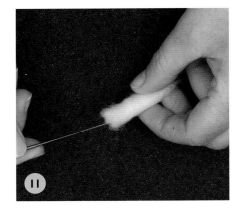

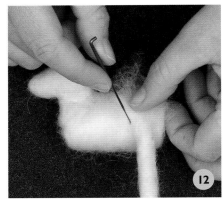

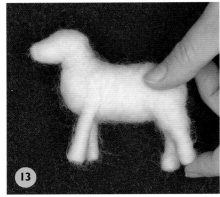

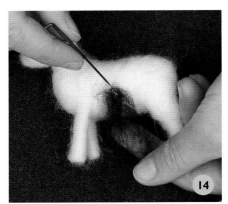

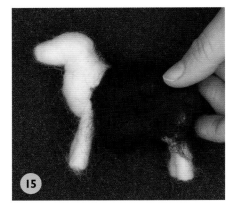

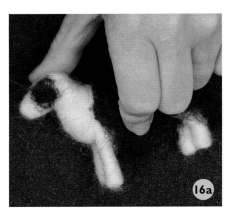

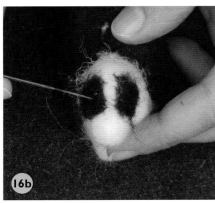

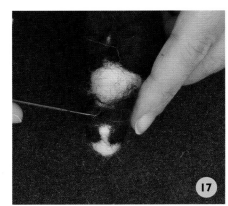

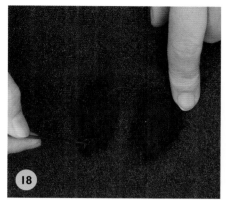

EARS

18. Fold a ½" (1.3 cm)-size piece of black wool into a triangle shape and needle it flat. Make two ears.

19. Lay the loose fibers of the triangle on the top side of the dog's head and needle to attach. Needle deeply at the center of the ear to help give it a natural curved look.

20. Needle some white wool onto the the back and sides of the neck. Add the wool in wisps and don't needle the whole piece down. The idea is to have the wool appear natural and hairlike.

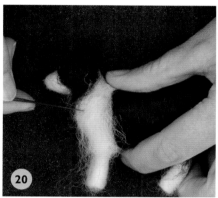

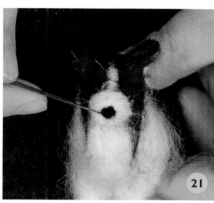

EYES, NOSE, AND MOUTH

21. Roll a tiny black ball and needle it onto the tip of the dog's snout.

22. Sew black beads onto the dog's face for eyes.

23. Needle a pinch of white wool behind the black beads so that the eyes will show.

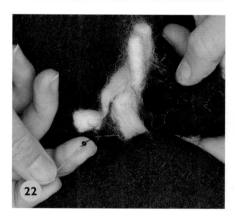

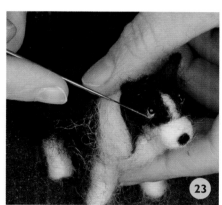

TAIL

24. Measure a 2" (5.1 cm)-long piece of black wool. Lay a pinch of white wool on the end, overlapping the black piece. Roll the piece lengthwise and needle to keep it from unrolling. Add more wool if the tail seems too thin.

25. Position the tail on the back of the dog's body and needle to attach.

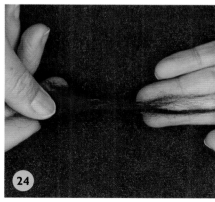

cat

Making needle-felted cats can be a challenge but if you recognize the proportions of the cat's body, it will be easier. The cat's head and snout are small. The limbs and body are slender. Keep these proportions in mind. This pattern makes a 2½" (6.4 cm)-tall cat.

MATERIALS

- 0.3 oz. (9 g) black wool
- small amount of white, yellow, and pink merino wool
- felting needle
- foam pad
- wooden skewer
- ruler

BODY

1. Measure a 7" × 2" (17.8 × 5.1 cm) piece of black wool.

2. Roll tightly into a 2" × 1" (5.1 × 2.5 cm) sausage shape. Needle the surface to keep the wool from unrolling.

HEAD

3. Measure a 4" × 1" (10.2 × 2.5 cm) piece of black wool.

4. Roll tightly into a ¾" (1.9 cm) round ball. Needle the surface to keep the ball from unrolling.

5. Wrap a wisp of black wool around your finger, then lay this neck piece on one end of the body. Needle the neck piece to the body. Position the head on top of the neck and needle around the edge of the head, through the neck, and into the body to form a secure attachment. Add more wool around the neck if the head seems too wobbly.

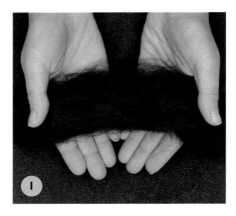
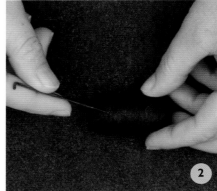
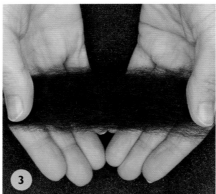
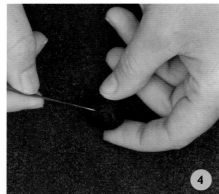

LEGS

6. Measure a 10" × 2" (25.4 × 5.1 cm) piece of black wool and divide it into four equal parts.

7. For each leg, begin by needling the wool into a flat shape. Turn the wool over and needle the opposite side flat and smooth.

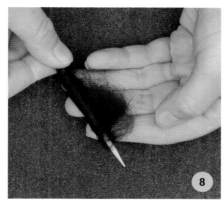

8. Tightly roll the flat piece of wool around the skewer. Leave the fibers loose at one end for attaching the leg to the body. Remove the leg from the skewer and needle to keep the leg from unrolling. Check to make sure that the leg is slender. If it seems too thick, pull some excess wool off of the end and roll the leg between the palms of your hands to help shrink it down. Needle the fibers from the outside edge towards the middle on the paw end of the leg. The leg should measure approximately 1¼" × ¼" (3.2 cm × 6 mm).

9. Repeat steps 6 through 8 with the other three legs.

ATTACHING THE LEGS TO THE BODY

10. Position the legs so that the loose fibers are halfway up on the cat's body. Needle the loose fibers into the side of the cat's body to secure the legs. Add more wool around the area of attachment and needle the area to shape and smooth.

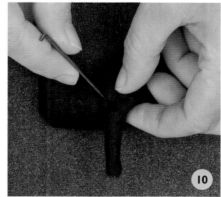

(continued)

11. The space between the front legs and back legs should measure about 1" (2.5 cm). Shape the legs and body by needling the underside of the cat's body. Keep in mind that the stomach area is usually more slender than the ribcage and chest.

EARS

12. Fold a small piece of black wool into a triangle shape. Needle the surface flat and leave the fibers loose at one end for attaching the ear to the head. Make two ears.

13. Position the ear on the cat's head and needle the loose fibers of the ear onto the head to attach. Repeat with the other ear.

14. Needle a pinch of pink wool into the center of each ear.

EYES

15. The cat's eyes are small and close together. Needle a small pinch of yellow wool on each side of the cat's face where the eyes will be. Shape the yellow wool into an oval as you are attaching it to the cat's face.

16. Needle a smaller pinch of black wool inside the yellow oval. Needle a tiny speck of white inside of the black.

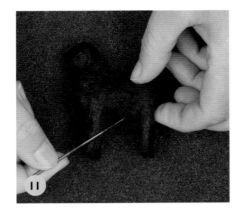

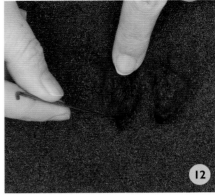

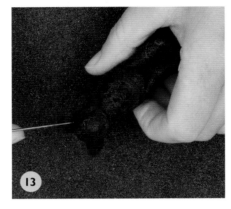

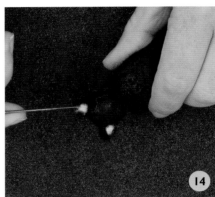

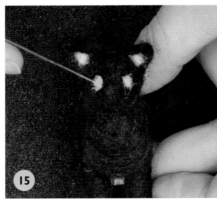

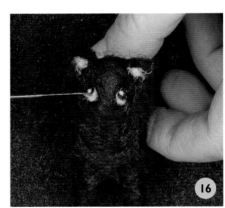

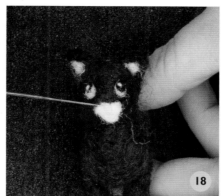

UPPER MOUTH

17. Roll two balls of white wool and needle onto the cat's face as indicated in the photo. Needle one more pinch of white wool onto the cat's face under the mouth for a chin.

18. Roll a piece of pink wool for the nose and needle it between the cat's upper lips.

TAIL

19. Roll a 4" × 1" (10.2 × 2.5 cm) piece of black wool on a skewer. Remove the tail and needle the surface to keep the wool from unrolling. Needle one end of the tail into a point and attach the loose fibers of the other end of the tail on the back end of the cat.

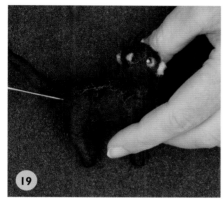

frog

Even though frogs aren't furry creatures you can still make a surprisingly realistic needle-felted frog. Use brightly colored wool for the body or contrasting colors for a spotted or striped frog.

MATERIALS

- 0.3 oz. (9 g) green (or desired color) wool
- small amount of gold, black, and white wool
- felting needle
- foam pad or other soft work surface
- wooden skewer
- ruler

BODY

1. Lay a strip of wool, approximately 8" × 2" (20.3 × 5.1 cm), on the foam pad. Starting at one end roll the strip of wool until it measures 2" (5.1 cm) long. Fold in the sides as you roll so the shape resembles a football. This piece needs to be firm. If it seems too soft, unroll what you have done and start all over.

2. Needle the surface of the body to keep it from unrolling. Set the body aside.

BACK LEGS

3. Fold a piece of wool into the size of a quarter. Needle the surface flat. Leave the fibers at one end loose, where the foot will attach to the leg.

4. Define the toes of the foot by needling an indentation between toes. Pull the toes out and twist the wool between your fingertips. Lift the foot off of the foam pad and needle on the other side of the foot.

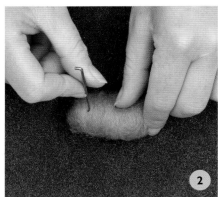

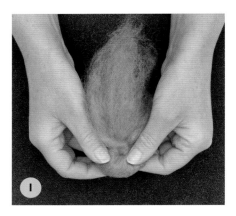

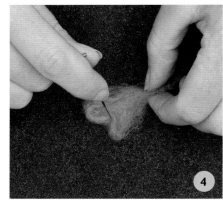

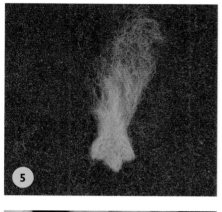

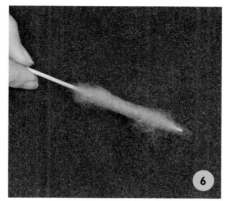

5. Keep the fibers loose at the end of the ankle.

6. Wrap a rectangular piece of wool about 2" (5.1 cm) long around the wooden skewer. Slide the wool off of the skewer.

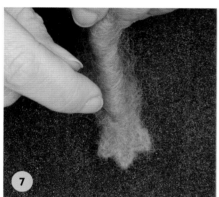

7. Lay the leg piece on top of the foot with the loose fibers overlapping. Needle at the ankle to attach. Pick up and needle the fibers from the outside edge of the ankle toward the middle.

8. Once the leg and foot are attached, roll the piece between the palms of your hands to help smooth the surface and create a stronger bond at the ankle. Leave the fibers at the top end of the leg loose for attaching to the body. Repeat steps 3 through 8 for the other leg.

ATTACHING AND POSITIONING THE LEGS

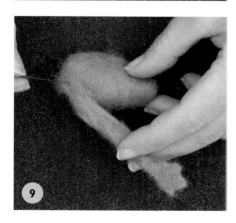

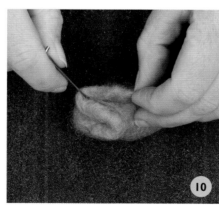

9. Lay the loose fibers of one of the legs along the back side of the frog's body. Needle the loose fibers onto the body.

10. Needle the thigh against the side of the body. Bend the leg at the knee and needle the calf against the body, beneath the thigh. Bend the leg at the ankle. Needle in place. Repeat with the other leg.

(continued)

11. Look at the frog from different angles and check to see if the legs are positioned the way you'd like. Reposition if desired.

FRONT LEGS

12. Make the front legs the same way as the back legs, but make the front legs about half of the size of the back legs. Make another ankle and foot.

ATTACHING THE FRONT LEGS TO THE BODY

13. Lay the loose fibers of the front leg above the back leg on the side of the body. Needle around the area of attachment, including the underarm.

14. Pull the front leg forward and lay the hand down. Needle to shape the arm in position. Repeat steps 13 and 14 for the other front leg.

15. Look at the frog from different angles to check for positioning. Reshape if desired.

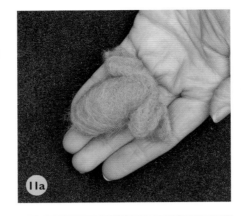

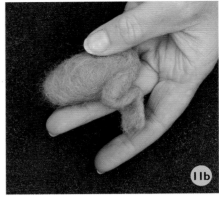

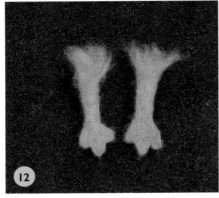

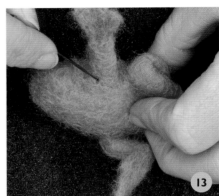

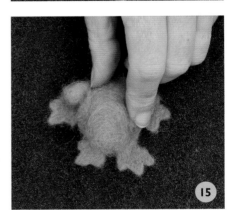

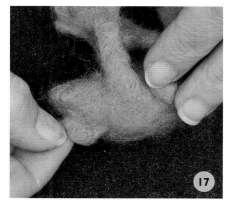

EYES AND MOUTH

16. Fold a piece of wool the size of a thumbnail into a ball. Leave the fibers loose at one end.

17. Lay the loose fibers of the ball on the side of the frog's head and needle to attach. This ball will be the base of the eye. Needle around the back and front of the eye, but don't needle it flat.

18. Needle a circle of gold wool into the center of the eye.

19. Needle a smaller circle of black wool within the gold.

20. Needle a speck of white wool on one edge of the black wool circle. Repeat steps 16 through 20 for the other eye.

21. Needle a thin strip of black wool where you want the mouth to be.

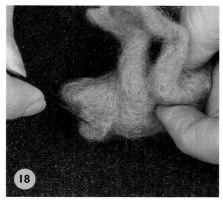

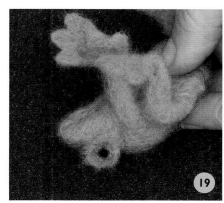

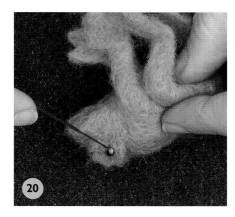

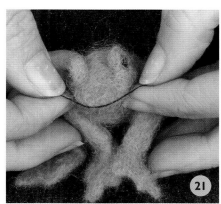

sheep

Sheep are fun to make because any type or color of wool will look adorable! Their round-barrel bodies are easy to adorn with a coat of curly locks. Try needle felting unspun mohair locks onto the sheep's body.

MATERIALS

- 0.3 oz. (9 g) white Romney wool
- a pinch of black and pink wool
- two beads
- sewing needle and black thread
- felting needle
- wooden skewer
- ribbon
- miniature brass bell
- foam pad or other soft work surface
- ruler

BODY, HEAD, AND NECK

1. Measure a 10" × 5" (25.4 × 12.7 cm) piece of white wool. Fold the sides in and roll a sausage shape about 2½" × 1½" (6.4 × 3.8 cm). Needle all over the surface to keep the wool from unrolling. Set the body aside.

2. Measure a 6" × 4" (15.2 × 10.2 cm) piece of wool and roll it into a cone shape about 1½" (3.8 cm) long. Needle all over the surface. The fibers should be loose at the wide end for attaching the head to the body.

3. Wrap a wisp of wool around your finger. This piece will be the neck and it will help fill the space between the head and the body.

4. Needle the neck on the top end of the body. Don't needle too much. Leave some loose wool around the neck.

5. Lay the head piece on top of the neck and needle the loose fibers of the head through the neck and into the

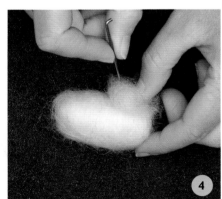

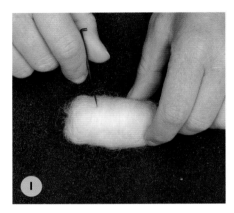
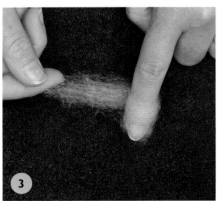

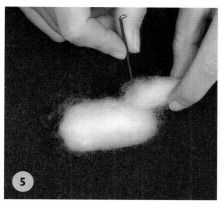

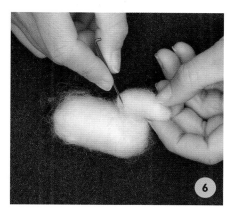

body. Needle all around the edge of the head to attach.

6. Position the head by gently lifting the snout while pulling down on the back of the head and neck. Hold the head in position with your thumb and needle around the head through the neck and into the body. Turn the body upside down and needle from underneath the body up through the neck and head.

7. Add some extra wool around the neck to fill the space between the head and body. Needle the whole surface of the sheep's body and head until you get the form you like.

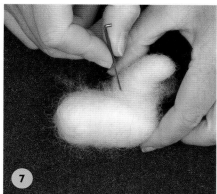

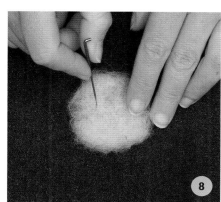

LEGS

8. Divide a 7" × 2" (17.8 × 5.1 cm) piece of wool into four equal parts, one for each leg. Fold one of the leg pieces in from the edges to make a round shape. Needle flat and turn the piece over. Needle the other side smooth.

9. Roll the leg piece tightly around a wooden skewer but keep the fiber on both ends of the leg loose.

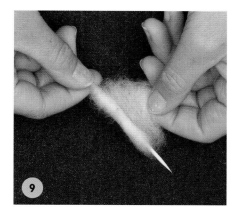

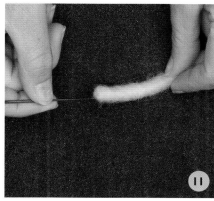

10. Slide the leg off of the skewer and needle the surface.

11. On one end of the leg, keep the fibers loose to attach to the body. On the opposite end, needle the fibers from the edge into the center and flatten into a hoof. Repeat steps 8 through 11 for the other three leg pieces.

(continued)

ATTACHING THE LEGS TO THE BODY

12. Lay one of the legs halfway up the rear of the body. Needle the loose fibers to attach.

13. Turn the sheep's body over and needle the leg from underneath. The leg should be firmly attached to the body. If it seems too floppy, add more wool around the inside of the leg. Needle the fibers.

14. Repeat steps 12 and 13 with the other three legs, adjusting placement as needed.

EARS

15. Fold a quarter-size piece of wool into a sheep's ear shape. Keep the fibers loose at one end for attaching the ear to the head.

16. Lay the sheep on its side and position the ear on the side of the head. Needle the loose fibers onto the side of the head.

17. Once the ear is attached, lay the ear on the edge of the foam pad and needle the inner, middle part of the ear to shape. Repeat steps 15 through 17 for the other ear.

EYES, NOSE, AND MOUTH

18. Thread a sewing needle with black thread and tie a knot at the end. Pick up a black bead with the needle and sew through the side of the sheep's head. Don't pull the needle all the way through.

19. Place the other black bead on the needle and pull the needle through the head. Sew back and forth through the beads and head a few times and pull to recess the beads slightly.

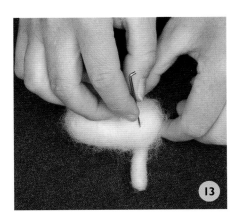

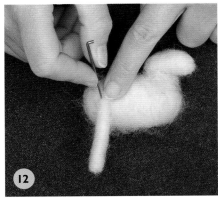

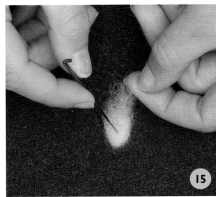

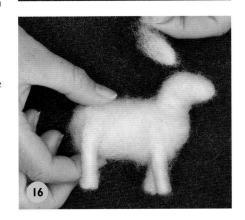

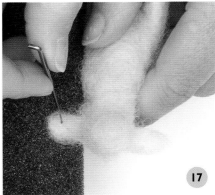

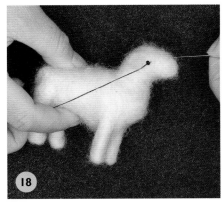

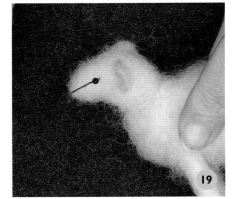

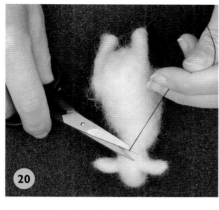

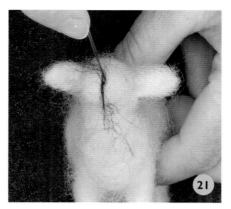

20. Once the beads are secure, sew the thread through the back of the head, tie it in a knot, and cut. Cover any visible thread with a pinch of white wool.

21. Lay a very thin strip of black wool down the middle of the sheep's nose. Needle the strip to the nose, keeping the top and bottom fibers loose.

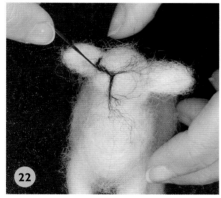

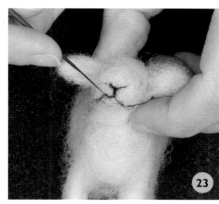

22. Split the fibers at the top of the nose to form a Y shape and needle them down. Snip off the extra wool at the end of the nostrils.

23. Split the fibers on the bottom of the nose to form an upside-down Y-shaped mouth. Snip off any excess fibers.

FINISHING TOUCHES

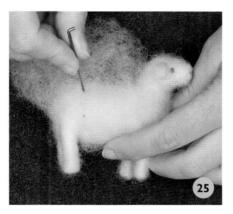

24. Needle a pinch of pink wool into the center of each ear.

25. Cover the sheep's body with a thin layer of white wool. The body should look fluffy and round.

26. Add some white wool to the sheep's chest to cover the area where the legs meet the body. Needle white wool on top of the sheep's head between the ears and down the back of the head to the neck. Needle a ball of wool onto the back of the sheep for a tail.

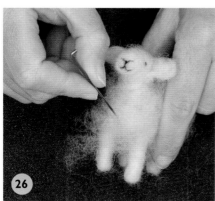

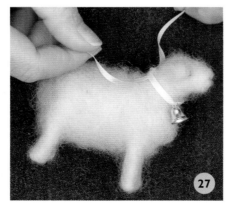

27. Thread the bell through the ribbon and tie around the sheep's neck.

pink pig

This little piggy is made in four parts. The pig's body, neck, head, and snout are all sculpted out of the same piece, so it is important to get the shape right at the beginning. After the main part of the pig is made, the legs, tail, and ears are added. This pattern makes a 4" (10.2 cm)-long pig.

MATERIALS

- 0.3 oz. (9 g) pink wool
- black beads for eyes
- wooden skewer
- sewing needle and thread

- felting needle
- foam pad
- ruler

BODY, HEAD, AND SNOUT OF PIG

1. Begin with a 10" × 2" (25.4 × 5.1 cm) piece of pink wool. Roll into a sausage shape about 2" (5.1 cm) long and needle the surface smooth.

2. Pinch one end of the sausage and gently pull. Needle this end to make a cone shape.

3. Wrap a layer of wool around the rest of the sausage shape. Needle the surface.

4. The cone shape is the pig's head and snout. Needle the end of the cone to define the shape of the snout. At the end of the snout, needle two deep holes for nostrils.

5. Needle on each side of the snout, up towards the pig's head. This will help define the pig's face.

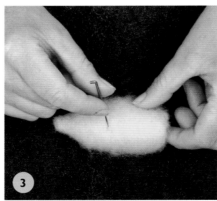
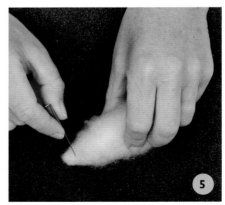
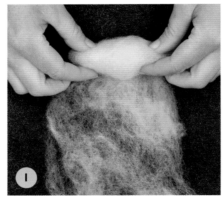
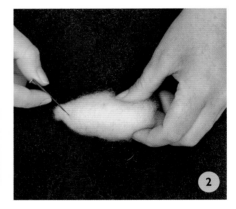

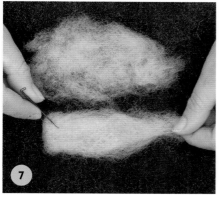

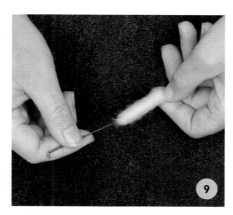

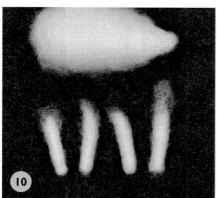

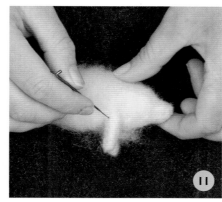

LEGS

Keep in mind that pigs have short, tiny legs despite their large bodies. You will need to make the legs dense so that they can support the body.

6. Divide a 10" × 3" (25.4 × 7.6 cm) piece of pink wool into four equal parts. These will be the legs.

7. For each leg, fold the piece of wool into a 1" (2.5 cm)-wide strip. Needle the surface of the wool.

8. Wrap the strip tightly around the wooden skewer.

9. Slide the leg off of the skewer and needle, keeping the fibers loose at one end for attaching to the body. Needle the other end of the leg flat for a hoof.

10. Repeat steps 7 through 9 for the other three legs.

ATTACHING THE LEGS TO THE BODY

11. Begin with the front legs. Position the leg on the side of the pig, halfway up the side of the body. Needle the loose fibers into the body.

(continued)

12. Use more wool just a pinch at a time, to pad the area around the attachment. Add wool to the inside of the leg and under the belly and add a little bit of wool at the shoulder. The idea is to make it look smooth and natural.

13. Repeat with the other front leg.

14. For the back legs, add a thigh to the legs by needling extra wool onto the top of the legs. A pinch or two should be enough.

15. Lay the thigh and leg on the side of the pig's body, on the rear end. The top of the thigh can almost reach the top of the pig's body.

16. Needle the thigh to the body. Add more wool to the area where the leg meets the underside of the body. Add a pinch or two of wool so that the leg, thigh, and body look smooth.

17. Repeat with the other back leg.

18. At this point, you may want to add a soft layer of pink wool to the pig's body to smooth it out, or if you think the pig should be a little fatter.

EARS

19. Fold a small piece of pink wool into a triangle and needle the surface. Lift it off the foam pad and needle the other side. Keep the fibers loose on one end to use for attachment to the head.

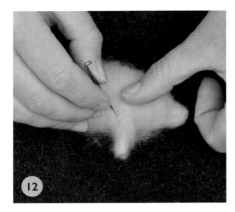

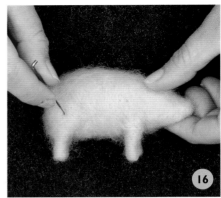

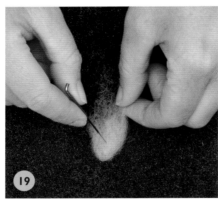

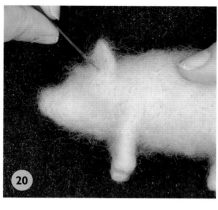

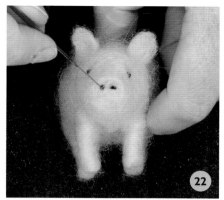

20. Decide where the ears will be and lay the loose fibers on the side of the pig's head. Needle the loose fibers to attach, and as you attach the ear, pull the base of the ear in to make a natural-looking fold.

21. Repeat with the other ear.

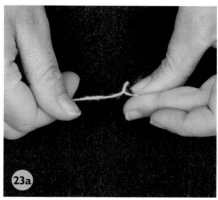

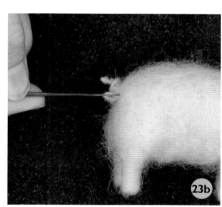

22. Sew black beads onto the face for eyes. Needle two specks of black wool on the snout for nostrils.

23. Curl a piece of pink wool by twisting it between your fingers. Needle the curl onto the back of the pig for a tail.

giraffe

This project is not difficult but it does take some time to add the brown wool spots onto the giraffe's body. Use photos of giraffes to help you decide where to put the spots. It is important to make the legs very firm and thin so that the giraffe won't need crutches! The giraffe in this project is 6" (15.2 cm) tall.

MATERIALS

- 0.3 oz. (9 g) tan or light brown wool
- 0.07 oz. (2 g) dark brown wool
- small amount white wool
- black beads for eyes
- felting needle
- foam pad
- wooden skewer
- ruler
- sewing needle and thread

BODY

1. Measure an 8" × 2" (20.3 × 5.1 cm) piece of light brown wool.

2. Roll tightly into a sausage shape that measures 2½" × 1½" (6.4 × 3.8 cm). Needle the surface to help keep the shape of the roll.

NECK

3. Measure a 5" × 2" (12.7 × 5.1 cm) piece of light brown wool.

4. Roll tightly into a 3" × 1" (7.6 × 2.5 cm) cone-shaped tube. Needle the surface to help hold the shape. Keep the fibers on both ends loose.

5. Attach the neck to the body by placing the loose fibers of the wide end of the neck onto the body.

6. Needle the loose fibers onto the neck to attach.

7. Add more light brown wool to the area where the neck connects with the body.

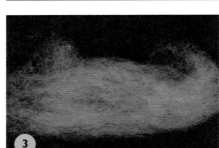

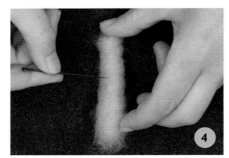

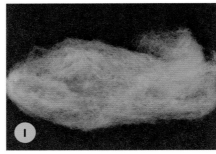

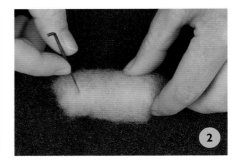

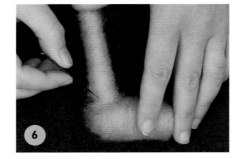

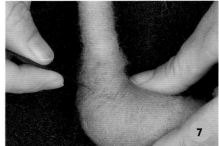

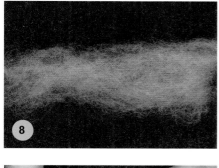

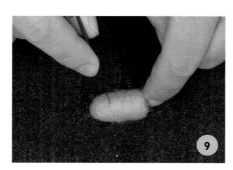

HEAD

8. Measure a 4" × 1" (10.2 × 2.5 cm) piece of light brown wool.

9. Roll tightly into a cone shape measuring 1" (2.5 cm) long. Needle the surface.

10. Lay the head onto the top of the neck and needle to attach.

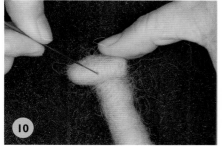

LEGS

11. For each leg, measure a 5" × 2" (12.7 × 5.1 cm) piece of light brown wool. Roll this piece tightly around the skewer.

12. Slide the wool off of the skewer and needle the surface. Keep the fibers on both ends loose. The leg should measure 2½" × ½" (6.4 × 1.3 cm).

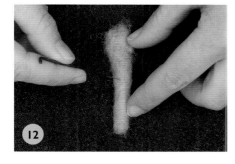

13. Wrap a small piece of white wool around the bottom half of the leg, ¾" (1.9 cm) long. Needle the white wool onto the leg.

14. Measure a 2" × 1" (5.1 × 2.5 cm) piece of light brown wool and loosely wrap it around the top of the leg to make a thigh. Needle the thigh to attach it to the leg. Repeat steps 11 through 14 with the other three legs.

ATTACHING THE LEGS TO THE BODY

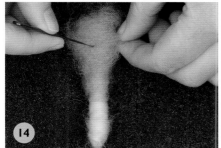

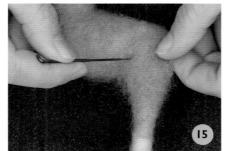

15. Lay the thigh of one of the legs on the side of the body. Needle the thigh onto the body. Add extra wool to the inner and outer thigh and needle to help create a firm attachment.

16. Repeat with the other three legs.

HOOVES

17. Needle a small circle of dark brown wool onto the bottom of the giraffe's legs to indicate hooves.

EARS, HORNS, AND TAIL

18. Fold a 1" (2.5 cm) piece of light brown wool into a narrow ear shape. Needle the ear and leave the fibers loose at one end to attach to the head. Make two.

19. Attach the ears to each side of the giraffe's head.

20. Add a pinch of dark brown wool to the inside of each ear.

21. Roll a pinch of light brown wool around the wooden skewer.

22. Slide the piece of wool off of the skewer and needle. This piece should measure ¼" (6 mm) long. Make 2.

23. Roll a very small pinch of dark brown wool into a ball and needle to the top of the light brown horn piece. Make two horns.

24. Needle the horns to the top of the giraffe's head, between the ears.

25. Roll a pinch of light brown wool between your fingers to make a thin, 2" (5.1 cm) long tail. Add dark brown wool to the end of the tail.

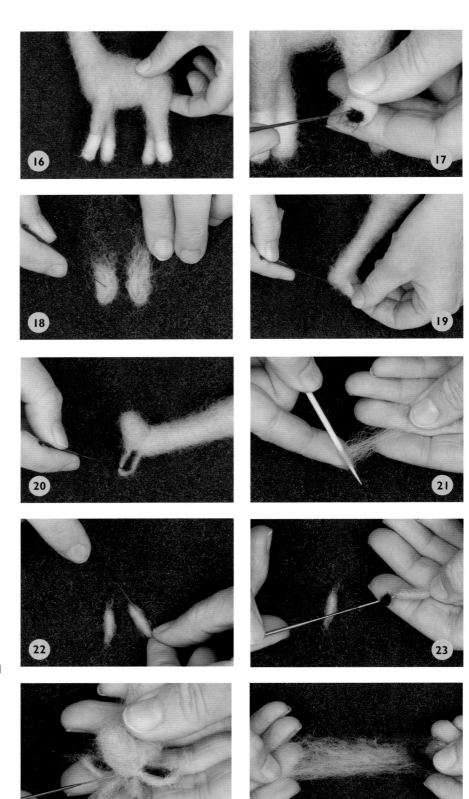

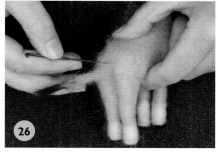

26. Attach the other end of the tail to the back of the giraffe.

SPOTS

27. Pull pieces of dark brown wool into little spots. Needle the spots onto the giraffe's body. Here are a few guidelines: Start at the top of the giraffe's neck with tiny spots and as you move down the neck, make the spots slightly larger. Also, the spots are smaller on the giraffe's legs than on the body.

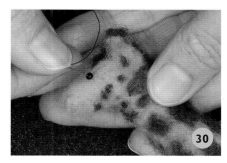

MANE

28. Roll a piece of dark brown wool between your fingertips and needle the mane to the giraffe, starting at the top of the head and going all the way down the neck.

29. Add a little bit of white wool to the giraffe's chest.

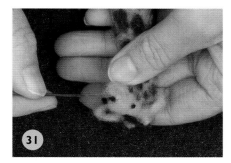

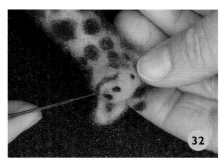

EYES AND MOUTH

30. Sew black beads onto either side of the giraffe's head for eyes.

31. Needle two spots of dark brown wool onto the end of the nose to indicate nostrils.

32. Add a strip of dark brown wool under the nostrils for a mouth.

mermaid

In this project, you will learn how to add details to a face using the felting needle and wool. Because it is so fine, merino wool is best to use. You can get creative with the mermaid hair color and style. Try using mohair locks, which are shiny and very curly.

MATERIALS

- 0.2 oz. (6 g) flesh-colored wool
- 0.2 oz. (6 g) green wool
- 0.2 oz. (6 g) curly wool locks
- pinch of black, white, and pink merino wool
- felting needle
- foam pad
- wooden skewer
- ruler

HEAD

1. Measure a 7" × 3" (17.8 × 7.6 cm) piece of flesh-colored wool.

2. Roll the wool tightly into a 1" (2.5 cm) ball. Needle the surface to keep the ball from unrolling and to help form the shape.

BODY

3. Measure a 10" × 3" (25.4 × 7.6 cm) piece of flesh-colored wool.

4. Roll tightly into a 2½" × 1½" (6.4 × 3.8 cm) sausage shape. Needle the surface.

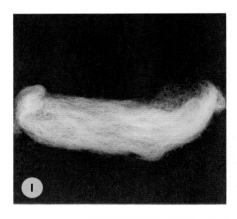

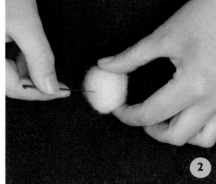

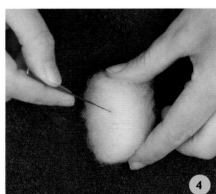

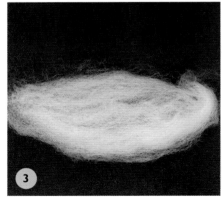

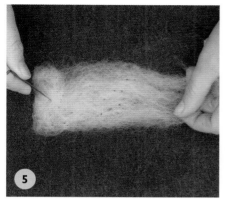

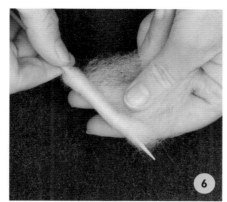

ARMS AND HANDS

5. Measure a 5" × 2" (12.7 × 5.1 cm) piece of flesh-colored wool and needle it flat.

6. Roll the piece tightly around a wooden skewer. Remove the arm and needle the surface. Keep the fibers loose at one end to help attach the arm to the body.

7. At the wrist end of the arm, create a hand by folding the wool and needling the fibers into an oval shape. Needle the area around the wrist so that it is narrower than the palm and finger area.

8. Make two arms.

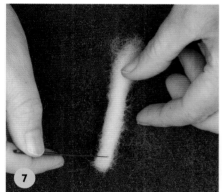

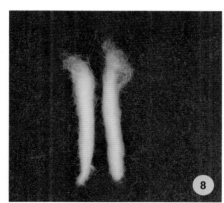

ATTACHING THE HEAD, TORSO, AND ARMS

9. Position the head on top of the body and needle around the edge to secure it in place. Add more flesh-colored wool around the neck and needle it smooth.

10. Position the arms on either side of the top part of the body and needle the loose fibers of the arms into the body to attach.

(continued)

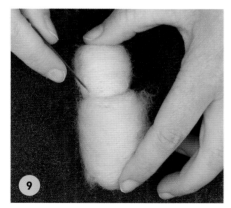

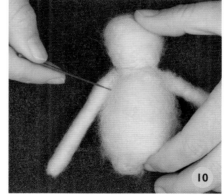

11. Add more flesh-colored wool around the shoulders and underarms and needle smooth.

TAIL

12. Measure a 10" × 3" (25.4 × 7.6 cm) piece of green wool.

13. Roll into a 4" × 2" (10.2 × 5.1 cm) cone shape. Needle the surface to keep the wool from unrolling.

14. One end of the tail shape is wider than the other. The wide end will be attached to the body.

FINS

15. Measure a 10" × 2" (25.4 × 5.1 cm) piece of green wool and split it in half. With each of the pieces, fold and needle the wool into a flat, oval shape with both ends tapered.

16. Needle the two pieces together at one end.

17. Attach the fins to the bottom of the tail on the narrow end.

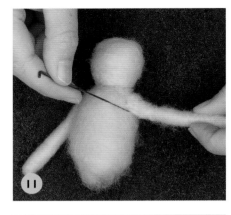

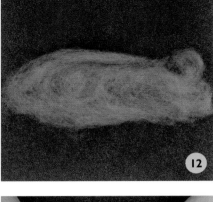

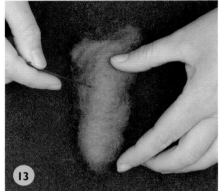

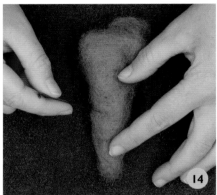

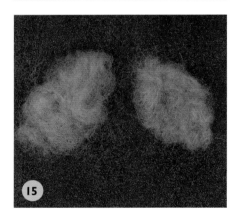

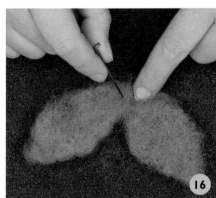

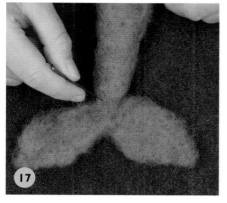

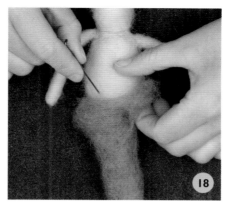

ATTACHING THE TAIL TO THE BODY

18. Place the body on top of the tail and needle the fibers of the body down into the tail.

19. Wrap a layer of green wool around the body and tail.

20. Needle the attachment area so that it is smooth and uniform.

FACE

21. Locate the midline on the face. The midline is a guide for positioning the nose and eyes. The eyes are on the midline and the nose is placed just below the midline. Needle a line across the face.

22. Roll a tiny piece of flesh-colored wool into a ball and needle it on the midline for a nose. Make sure it is not too large.

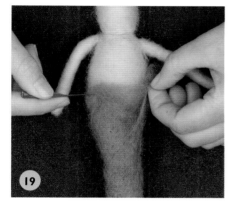

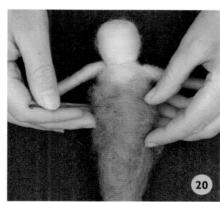

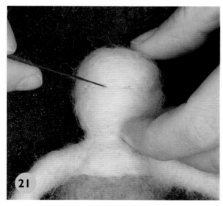

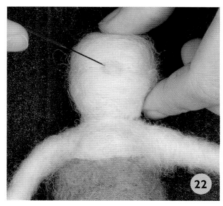

23. Needle a mouth line onto the face below the nose.

24. Add a strip of black wool onto the line for a mouth.

25. Roll a pinch of pink wool and needle it under the black line for lips.

26. Roll two small ovals with the white merino wool and position them on the face on either side of the nose on the midline. Needle on the white wool.

27. Roll a smaller piece of black merino wool and needle it into the center of the eye, but make sure the black connects to the edge of the eye in a spot or it will look like your mermaid is staring. Needle a small piece of black wool from the inner edge of the eye around the top to the outside edge.

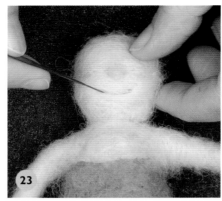

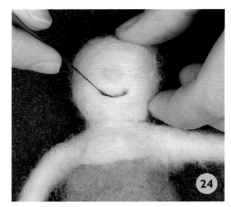

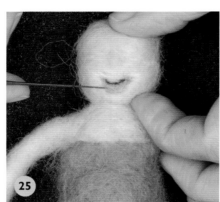

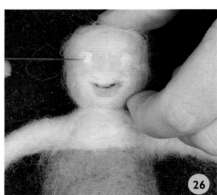

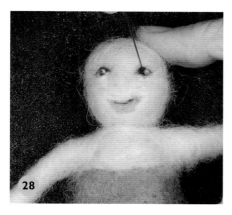
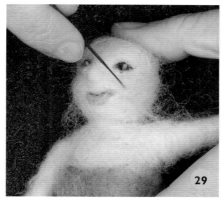

28. Roll a very small piece of white merino wool into a ball and needle it into the black part of the eye.

29. Needle a pinch of pink wool onto the cheeks.

HAIR

30. Starting at the center top of the head, needle the blunt end of the wool lock into the head and leave the rest of the lock loose. Add more locks, moving from the inside center of the head outward.

31. When the head is full of curly locks, you can shape the hair by needling it down in parts and keeping it loose and wild in other parts.

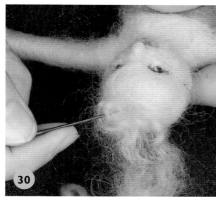

gnome girl

This pattern can be followed to create a variety of small figures. With shorter hair, this gnome girl could become a gnome boy. Give your figure curly white locks and a beard and you'll have their grandpa! Any color of wool can be used to make clothing, shoes, and a hat. Use your imagination to change the figure into an elf or fairy. The figure is 4" (10.2 cm) tall; 7" (17.8 cm) including the hat.

MATERIALS

- 0.04 oz. (1 g) flesh-colored wool
- 0.04 oz. (1 g) yellow wool
- 0.07 oz. (2 g) red wool
- small amount of gray wool
- small amount of white, black, and red merino wool
- brown wool locks for hair
- felting needle
- foam pad
- wooden skewer
- ruler

HEAD

1. Measure an 8" × 2" (20.3 × 5.1 cm) piece of flesh-colored wool.

2. Roll tightly into a 1¼" (3.2 cm) round ball. Needle the ball to keep the wool from unrolling.

BODY AND LEGS

3. Measure a 4" × 2" (10.2 × 5.1 cm) piece of red wool. Lightly needle the surface. Roll the wool around the wooden skewer, slide it off, and needle the surface so the wool doesn't unroll. Leave the fibers at both ends loose.

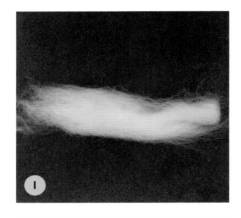

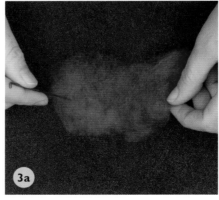

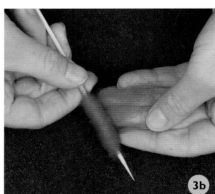

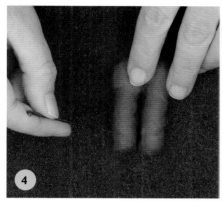

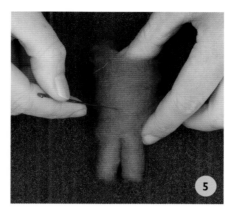

4. The leg should measure 2½" (6.4 cm) long. Make two.

5. To make the body, lay the legs side by side and wrap a 1" (2.5 cm)-wide strip of red wool around the top half of the legs so that they are wrapped together.

6. Needle to secure the wool in place.

ATTACHING THE HEAD TO THE BODY

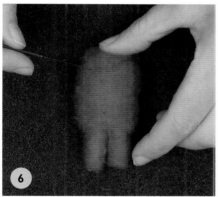

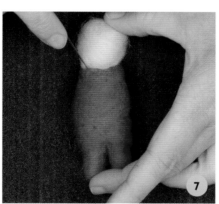

7. Place the head on top of the body and legs. If it seems that the body needs to be thicker, wrap another layer of red wool around the body and needle it smooth before attaching the head. Needle the fibers from the bottom of the head into the body to attach. Turn the gnome upside down and needle the red wool from the body into the head to help form a more secure attachment. Add more red wool around the neck area if the head seems too floppy.

ARMS

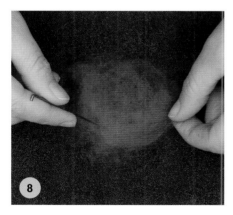

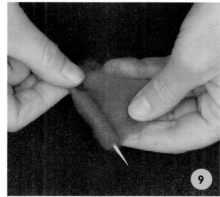

8. Measure a 3" × 2" (7.6 × 5.1 cm) piece of red wool and needle the surface flat. Turn the piece over and needle the other side flat.

9. Roll the flat piece of red wool on a skewer. Slide the wool off of the skewer and needle to keep the fibers from unrolling. Keep the fibers loose at both ends. The arm should measure 1½" (3.8 cm) long.

(continued)

10. Make two arms.

ATTACHING THE ARMS TO THE BODY

11. Position the shoulder of the arm on the side of the body and needle the loose fibers all around to attach. Adjust the placement of the arm if necessary.

12. Repeat with the other arm on the opposite side.

13. Add a cushion of red wool around the shoulder and underarm and needle to create a smooth attachment.

HANDS

14. Fold a dime-sized piece of flesh-colored wool in a flat oval. Needle the surface of the hand to hold the shape. Leave the fibers loose at the wrist end for attaching the hand to the arm. Make two hands.

15. Position the hand at the bottom of the arm and needle the fibers of the hand to the arm.

16. Repeat with the other hand.

DRESS

17. Measure a 3" × 2" (7.6 × 5.1 cm) piece of red wool and needle the surface flat and smooth. Leave the fibers on the sides and top loose for attaching the dress.

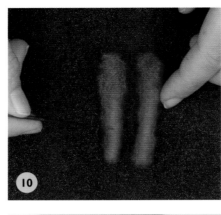

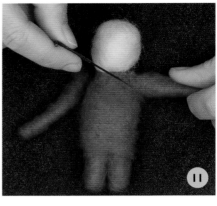

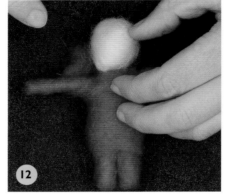

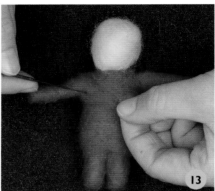

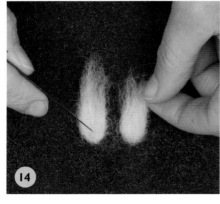

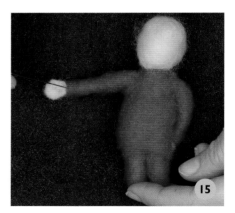

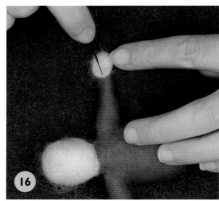

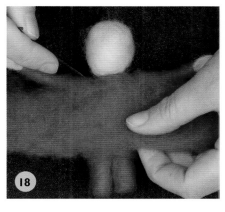

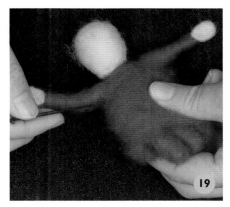

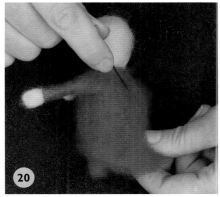

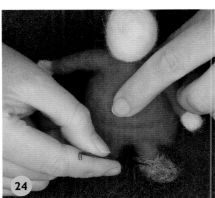

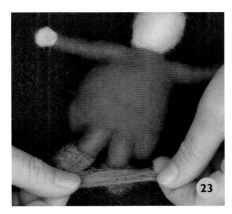

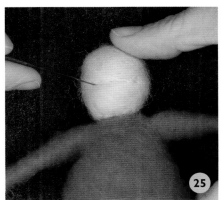

18. Lay the dress on the gnome girl's body and begin to attach at the neck.

19. Lift up the arms and needle under the arms and around the back of the neck.

20. Overlap the sides of the dress in back and needle the loose fibers to make a seam for the dress.

SHOES

21. Fold a 1" (2.5 cm) square piece of gray wool into a ¾" (1.9 cm) flat oval shape. This will be the sole of the shoe. Make two.

22. Needle the flat oval shape to the bottom of the legs.

23. Wrap a strip of gray wool around the top of the soles and around to the back of the legs, where the back of the shoe and heel are. Needle to secure the wool in place. Use the photo as a guide. Repeat with the other shoe.

24. Turn the gnome girl upside down and needle the bottom of the shoes flat.

FACE

25. Lightly needle a line across the middle of the gnome girl's face.

(continued)

26. To make a nose, roll a pea-sized ball of flesh-colored wool and needle it onto the middle of the face below the midline.

27. On each side of the nose, needle a pinch of white wool into an oval shape for eyes.

28. Needle a smaller black circle within the white.

29. Needle a thin black line onto the eyelid.

30. Add a speck of white in the black.

31. Needle a short line, just below the nose, where the mouth should be located. Needle a strip of black wool onto the line to add depth for a mouth.

32. Add a small piece of red wool under the mouth for lips.

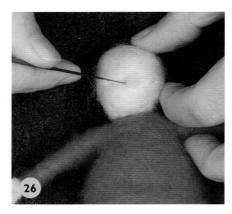

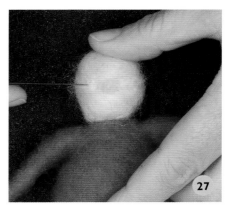

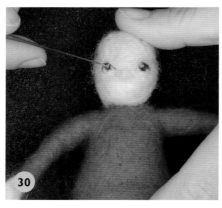

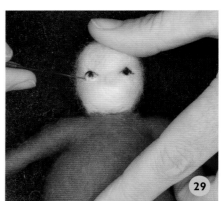

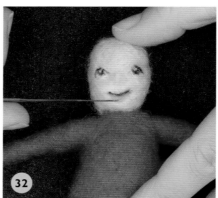

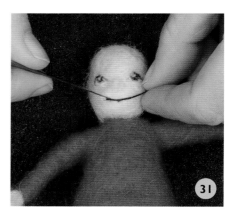

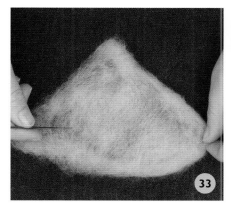

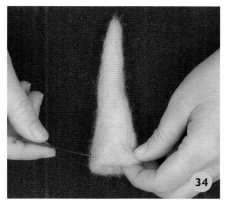

CAP

33. Measure a 3" (7.6 cm) square piece of yellow wool. Needle the surface and fold the sides in to make a triangle shape. Turn the wool over and needle the other side.

34. Roll the triangle into a cone shape and needle the sides together.

35. The cap should be 3½" (8.9 cm) tall and fit snugly on the gnome girl's head. Needle the edge of the cap to the head all the way around to attach it to the top of the head.

36. Take a few brown locks of wool and tuck one end of the lock up into the cap and needle the cap over it to secure. Do the same on the other side of the gnome girl's head. Tuck a few locks of wool under the front of the hat and needle to hold in place.

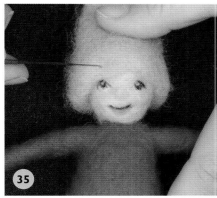

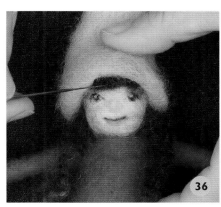

gallery

resources

Spark Fiber Arts
Fine Fiber Studio
101 SE Jefferson St.
Albany, OR 97321
1.541.926.1095
www.sparkfiberarts.com
great resource for events related to needle felting, sources, books, and links to other felt artists

Birgitte Krag Hansen
Bjergmarken 50
4300 Holbæk
Denmark
www.feltmaking.com
wonderful artists with very inspirational website; excellent books on how to needle-felt figures and animals

A Child's Dream Come True
1223-D Michigan St.
Sandpoint, ID 83864
1.800.359.2906
www.achildsdream.com
needle-felting kits and supplies

Weir Dolls and Crafts
4125 Jackson Rd.
Ann Arbor, MI 48103
1.888.205.5034
www.weirdollsandcrafts.com
natural fiber crafts, fabrics, felts, and rovings

FeltCrafts
P.O. Box 5887
Woodland Park, CO 80866
www.feltcrafts.com
feltmaking supplies, felt craft kits, needle-felting machine and supplies, and wet felting machines and supplies

Blue Goose Glen
1.800.941.2556
a wide variety of fibers for spinning, dyeing, and felting

Outback Fibers
From the Wool Shed
312 Oak Plaza Cove
Georgetown, TX 78628
1.800.276.5015
www.outbackfibers.com
specializing in fine Australian merino wool roving, silk, felting fiber, and wool batts

Halcyon Yarn
12 School St.
Bath, ME 04530
1.800.341.0282
www.halcyonyarn.com
an extensive selection of yarn and fibers, books, videos, and equipment for knitting, spinning, weaving, and other fiber arts

Harrisville Designs
41 Main St.
P.O. Box 806
Harrisville, NH 03450
1.800.338.9415
www.harrisville.com
products for the weaving and knitting enthusiast, as well as the Friendly Loom line of educational toys for children, made in their own mills in Harrisville, New Hampshire

Northeast Fiber Arts Center
1.802.288.8081
www.northeastfiberarts.com
fibers, needle-felting hat forms, mats, learn-to-felt kits, needle holders, and much more

Woolpets
Laurie Sharp
19566 Augusta Ave. N.E.
Suquamish, WA 98392
1.360.930.0942
www.woolpets.com
needle-felting kits and supplies

about the author

Laurie Sharp is a full-time artist and has been needle felting for over five years. She raises her own sheep, and shears and processes the wool for most of her projects. She has been featured on HGTV's *That's Clever!* Her work has been shown in a number of galleries in the Pacific Northwest where she lives with her husband and business partner, Kevin Sharp. As a professional photographer, Kevin took all the photos for the book and also photographs the steps for needle-felting kits that Laurie sells from her website www.woolpets.com.

acknowledgment

Thanks to our friend Sarah Evans for helping us edit the material.